The Meaning of History

The Meaning of History

With a new introduction by
Maria Nemcova Banerjee

Nikolai Berdyaev

Transaction Publishers
New Brunswick (U.S.A.) and London (U.K.)

New material this edition copyright © 2006 by Transaction Publishers, New Brunswick, New Jersey. Originally published in 1936 by Geoffrey Bles. Introduction first published in *Modern Age*, Summer 2004.

This book is printed on acid-free paper that meets the American National Standard for Permanence of Paper for Printed Library Materials.

Library of Congress Catalog Number: 2005055994
ISBN: 1-4128-0497-3
Printed in the United States of America

Library of Congress Cataloging-in-Publication Data

Berdiaev, Nikolai, 1874-1948.
　[Smysl istorii. English]
　The meaning of history / Nikolai Berdyaev ; with a new introduction by Maria Nemcova Banerjee.
　　　p. cm.
Originally published: London : G. Bles, 1936. With new introd.
Includes bibliographical references.
　　ISBN 1-4128-0497-3 (alk. paper)
　　1. History—Philosophy. 2. Christianity—Philosophy. I. Title.

D16.8B326　2006
901—dc22　　　　　　　　　　　　　　　　　2005055994

CONTENTS

INTRODUCTION TO THE TRANSACTION EDITION

NIKOLAI BERDYAEV AND SPIRITUAL
FREEDOM

"Victory over death-bearing time has been the fundamental theme of my life," says Berdyaev in the introduction to his *Spiritual Autobiography*.[1] Composed during the last decade of his life, this retrospective narrative is, like everything that Berdyaev wrote, an essay in philosophical meditation. In his conception, memory is much more than the faculty of passive recollection. Instead, the act of remembrance seizes up the meaning of the lived past in a moment of creative vitality, assessing it in the urgency of a consciousness in contact with the eternal.

Born in an aristocratic family in Kiev, Nikolai Berdyaev (1874-1948) lived through the cataclysmic events of the first half of a century whose aftershocks still haunt us. Witness to two world wars, he observed the destruction of established cultures in the traumatic birth of new worlds, having experienced three Russian revolutions from close-up. Four times arrested on political suspicion, first by the Imperial and then by the Bolshevik police, he died an exile after years of intense intellectual activity, at a philosophical distance from actuality. He was never more than a curious but unwelcome guest in history. He fearlessly engaged it on the level of ideas while remaining alien to its means and ends, gifted with an incurable longing for transcendence.

The awareness of a spiritual realm beyond the mundane bustle of existence came early to Berdyaev. Characteristically, he first apprehended it in the dialectical moment of negation, as the pain of a lack. "The sense of having fallen into an inferior world was more familiar to me," is how he puts it.[2] He admits to being unable to recall an experience of religious conversion, when the void of spirit was suddenly made full. But he singles out one ecstatic, soaring instant of transformation, which he marks as the initiation into his lifelong philosophical quest for spiritual freedom:

> I remember a moment—it was summer in the country—I found myself in the garden, at the hour of twilight and my heart was heavy.... Under the clouds, night was growing thicker, but suddenly a light surged inside me. I do not call this moment a "conversion," because I was in no way a sceptic before that, nor a materialist, or an atheist, not even an agnostic—and because even afterwards, my inner contradictions persisted; the perfection of inner peace did not follow from it and the anguish caused by complex religious problems did not cease. To give a true picture of my spiritual path, I must insist on freedom, as the origin and the end of my religious life.[3]

In biographical retrospect, Berdyaev's intellectual trajectory seems marked by a recurrent pattern of withdrawal from an established mode of being, a rupture followed by a surge of creativity. At the age of twenty, his mental exit from the aristocratic world of his family tradition was linked to his first encounter with Marxism. It was a philosophical worldview he would revisit critically at various points in his career.

But even in his youthful enthusiasm, he was not convinced by the systematic exposition of dialectical materialism as such. Rather, he responded to the winds of freedom he sensed blowing in the revolutionary élan of the Social Democrats he met. He was in tune with the cosmopolitan outlook of their intellectual exponents, many of whom were Jewish. And instinctively, he shared their opposition to capitalism, which he associated with the dead weight of bourgeois culture.

While insisting on social justice for the oppressed classes, Berdyaev maintained that a political revolution could at best bring only an incomplete liberation. Precocious and exceptionally well read, the twenty-year-old thinker understood that matter and all that pertains to it is essentially conservative. In debating the materialistic theses of Marxism within the Social Democratic gatherings in Kiev, he was taking on the impossible task of grafting spiritual sight onto the blind, toiling, still subterranean mole of history.

Berdyaev's withdrawal from the arena of politics coincided with his move to St. Petersburg in the summer of 1904. There he plunged into the dionysiac whirl of the Russian Silver Age and its rich literary culture. He became familiar with the leading personalities of Russian Symbolism, visionary poets like Alexander Blok, Andrei Bely, and Viacheslav Ivanov, who propounded the doctrine of theurgic art. But of all of them, he was most fascinated by the originality and the verbal power of the essayist Vasili Rozanov. And yet, the latter's conception of Christ as a lunar being who had made the fruits of this world taste bitter, was alien to him.

Soon enough Berdyaev would feel oppressed by the overwrought sensuality of the artistic milieu. He grew tired of the febrile discussions of Christianity and the impending apocalypse, which had first drawn him to the salon of Zinaida Gippius and Dmitri Merezhkovsky. Having initiated the series of lectures at the "Philosophical-Religious Society" with the topic "Christ and the World," he gave up as futile the project of reconciling the Petersburg cultural elite with the more open-minded representatives of the Orthodox Church. For his part, he went on to explore the deep roots of Russian messianism by keeping company with a variety of God-Seekers among the common people.

The failure of the Revolution of 1905, with the pathos of roused but ill-led masses, moved Berdyaev to the quick. That debacle led him and other disenchanted intellectuals to a crisis of consciousness that culminated with the publication of *Vekhi* (*Landmarks*) in 1909. Berdyaev and his friend, Sergei Bulgakov, with whom he had collaborated in publishing the philosophical and religious reviews *Novyi Put'* (*The New Path*) and *Voprosy Zhizni* (*Life Questions*), were the prime movers behind this effort.

Vekhi is a collection of essays, presenting an ideologically coherent attempt to analyze and demystify the mentality and the values of the Russian revolutionary intelligentsia. Its publication caused an immediate stir. Some saw it as a showpiece and an apology for the liberal spirit of compromise in matters of politics and social formation. Lenin denounced it in the crudest of terms.

Berdyaev's lead essay, "Philosophical Truth and the Moral Truth of the Intelligentsia,"[4] initiates the discussion on a high philosophical note. It can be read as the seminal first sketch for all of his future meditations about the spirit of Russian Communism. In 1909, with the future of Russia still being weighed on the scales of history, Berdyaev's diagnosis sounded more cautionary than prophetic.

With admirable pith and clarity, Berdyaev lays bare the poverty and the narrowness of thought embedded in the culture of several generations of Russian radicalism, from Belinsky to the Marxists. He discloses a virulent strain of pseudo-religious beliefs, barely concealed under the professions of atheism that united the various factions of that schismatic sect. The prime example of this is the elevation of the moral imperative of social justice as the highest category of truth (*pravda*), above and beyond the criteria of intellectual integrity associated with truth as *veritas*. He attributes this root phenomenon to "the orientation of their will," rather than to a defect in thinking.[5]

But in his conclusion, Berdyaev mitigates his indictment of the misguided rebels by laying the blame squarely on those who still held the reins of power in Russia and ruled it in the name of a debased version of Christianity. He writes: "The Russian intelligentsia has been what Russian history has made it. The sins of our morbid history, of our historical system of government, and of eternal reaction are reflected in its psychological make–up."[6] It is a very self-revealing assessment, showing Berdyaev's irreducible sympathy for the gesture of human liberation, no matter how flawed. It also raises the question of responsibility for the evils in Russian society from the arena of politics to a meta-historical level.

As Berdyaev saw it, the course of historical Christianity, with its sins of omission and commission, can be traced back to its fall away from Christ and His gift of freedom into the trap of the temporal world. That conversion of freedom into necessity is perennially repeated in the tragic fate of creativity in human culture, which reifies every inspired act into an objective value or, worse still, degrades it into a commodity. Formed in the crucible of his personal experience of Christianity, the tragic sense of life is fundamental to Berdyaev's philosophical outlook. But unlike for Nietzsche, who shared that sense with him, it is not an aesthetic but a spiritual value.

In Berdyaev's conception, the advent of Christianity was not a historical but a metaphysical event. In his coming, Christ tore the curtain of human time asunder, and from across that rupture, which is also an opening to the eternal, He calls for a creative response from each individual. Thus raised, the question of Man-God is the central theme of Berdyaev's philosophy. He returns to it again and again in manifold variations throughout his writings. It is the pivotal nexus linking his insight into spiritual freedom with his eschatolgical meditations on human destiny in this world.

The identification of Christ with the mystery of human freedom brought Berdyaev into an intimate dialogue with Fyodor Dostoevsky, the visionary novelist whom he regards as the greatest of Russian thinkers. Indeed, he confided that his personal image of the Christ was formed in the likeness of the figure Dostoevsky conjured up, stepping out of eternity into the deserted square in Seville to stand face to face with the Grand Inquisitor.

Like Alyosha, Berdyaev reads "The Legend of the Grand Inquisitor" from the point of view of faith, as a poem in praise of Christ. And similarly, he also understands that Ivan, the youthful author of the poem, is on the side of the old ascetic with despair in his heart and contempt for the pitiful human specimen on his lips. In the Grand Inquisitor chapter of his brilliant study, *Dostoevsky*, he writes: "It is noteworthy that the extremely powerful vindication of Christ [which is what the Legend is] should be put into the mouth of the atheist Ivan Karamazov. It is indeed a puzzle, and it is not clear on the face of it which side the speaker is on and which side the writer; we are left free to interpret and to understand for ourselves: that which deals with liberty is addressed to the free."[7]

As he explains in his *Spiritual Autobiography,* the book on Dostoevsky originated in the lectures he gave at the Writers' Union in Moscow during the winter of 1920-21.[8] It was a time when the Soviet regime was still consolidating its grip on power and the implementation of the Bolshevik doctrine had not yet achieved Shigalev's logical rigor. Brave voices from the recent past could still be heard at random, in nooks and crannies behind the official façade of Revolution.

Berdyaev opened the lecture series with a meditation on "The Legend of the Grand Inquisitor," which he called "the high point of Dostoevsky's work and the crown of his dialectics."[9] It goes unsaid that the events unfolding in the theater of history, with their grim conversion of liberation into enslavement and the trading of freedoms for bread, provided an existential subtext for Berdyaev's reading of that dramatic poem. He argues that Dostoevsky's conception of freedom is what lends such power and also the cruel edge to the novelistic situations into which he casts his rebellious characters. In Berdyaev's own words: "He was 'cruel' because he would not relieve man of his burden of freedom, he would not deliver him from suffering at the price of such a loss, he insisted that man must accept an enormous responsibility corresponding to his dignity as a human being."[10]

The discussion of the psychological and the moral dilemma posed by the choice between freedom and compassion in chapter III ("Freedom") and chapter IV ("Evil") of his *Dostoevsky* is central to Berdyaev's understanding of the novelist's spiritual universe. But it can also serve as an intellectual key to unlock the

[xiii]

core of his own philosophical quest. In this double exposure, Berdyaev's reading of Dostoevsky's texts shows him at his best, disclosing his inner self in a dialogue of freedom within the aura of the eschatological Christ. It was that dialogue of faith Alyosha had offered, only to be rebuffed by Ivan.

Above all, Berdyaev insists on releasing freedom from the constraints of morality as codified by society's laws. Nor does he accept a definition of freedom that reduces it to being an arbiter of the choice between good and evil, in the objective sphere of rationality. For Berdyaev, this "liberty of conscience," which European humanism claimed as its signal value, is merely "a material liberty."[11] But even though it may only offer a partial liberation, this "first freedom" must be defended on its own level. By contrast, spiritual freedom vaults above the objective order of human morality. "Freedom cannot be identified with goodness or truth or perfection: it is by nature autonomous, it is freedom, and not goodness."[12]

That radical disjunction between freedom and morality has deep roots in early Christian thought. Long before Dostoevsky and Berdyaev, Saint Augustine had distinguished between two types of freedom—the freedom within the law (*libertas minor*) and the freedom beyond it (*libertas maior*). The first acknowledges the primacy of reason in the *praxis* of choosing between good and evil; the second emanates from Divine Grace and, as such, it operates beyond the scope of rationality.

As Berdyaev sees it, Dostoevsky's originality lies in the way he recast the Augustinian problem of two freedoms by approaching it from the human rather than from the divine side. In his own intellectual transcript, Dostoevsky's agonistic dialogue between Man and God emerges in the form of a paradox: "Free goodness, which alone is true, entails the liberty of evil."[13] In Dostoevsky's fictional world the existential path of amoral characters like Svidrigailov and Stavrogin illustrates the negative side of the conundrum. Starting with unlimited freedom, they experiment with all forms of evil and end up with the destruction of their own freedom, "its degeneration into an evil necessity."[14]

Closing in on the paradoxical circle of his argument, Berdyaev goes on to say: "On the other hand, the denial of the freedom of evil in favor of an exclusive freedom of good ends equally in a negation of freedom and its degeneration into a good necessity. But good necessity is not good, because goodness resides in freedom from necessity."[15]

The "good necessity" is the ostensible option advocated by the Grand Inquisitor. The logic of that choice excludes the living Christ from all the transactions of human history, replacing Him by a fraudulent authority that promises miracles of compassion in His name. Unlike his counterparts on the podium of Soviet actuality, the aged cardinal of the Roman Church understands that man does not live by bread alone. After all, Ivan, who authored the poem, is heir to the pseudo-theological mentality of the Russian radical intelligentsia. That is why the Grand Inquisitor commutes Christ's death sentence to an ambiguous formula of dismissal: "Go and come no more."[16]

The dilemma of choosing between freedom and compassion cannot be resolved within the parameters set up by the Euclidean mind. In the prologue to his fantastic poem, Ivan had trained the sharp edge of his either/or logic on the problem of unjustified suffering. His formulation of it may be encoded in the reductionist style of the Russian 1860s, but the question he raises is an ancient one. It has gnawed at the heart of every attempt to construct a philosophical theodicy. Of course, Ivan is no theologian and his purpose for revisiting the theme is strictly deconstructive. In arguing the case of outraged humanity, he is performing a symbolic tyrannicide against God the Creator, an effigy of power he has erected in *imago patri*. The procedures of his prosecutorial logic imitate those of revolutionary terror. God stands impeached for allowing the suffering of innocent children to run unchecked throughout human history. In Ivan's tribunal, He will be convicted on the mutually contradictory charges of impotence and abuse of power.

Berdyaev reads Dostoevsky's work in all its complexity as one continuous, spiritually intense struggle to answer Ivan's arguments. His novelistic version of theodicy, just like Berdyaev's own philosophical *praxis*, begins and ends with the attempt to justify the human personality in the light of Christ's mysterious gift of freedom. Berdyaev writes: "I would sum it up in a paradoxical form, thus: The existence of evil is proof of the existence of God. If the world consisted wholly and uniquely of goodness and righteousness there would be no need for God, for the world itself would be God. God is, because evil is. And that means that god is because freedom is."[17]

Throughout his life, Berdyaev has resisted and rejected Ivan's anthropomorphic conception of God as power. He consistently refutes the idea that the divine can be derived from or linked to any form of secular or social authority. "God is less powerful than a policeman," he says in his *Autobiography*.[18] For Berdyaev, God the Son was always closer to his mind and heart than God the Progenitor. Only a suffering God could reconcile him to the evidence of undeserved suffering in this world. The relation between the human and the divine, as Berdyaev encodes it in his metaphysical gloss on Christ's message of salvation, is not one of power but of reciprocity. Only love in its

[xvi]

pure form as spiritual energy gives a human meaning to the true dialectics of higher freedom.

Even though Berdyaev welcomes the passing of the Russian Empire, the revolution born of the war brought him no joy. Already in 1916, in political debates with members of the Socialist Revolutionary Party and the Left Cadets, he had talked about the impending revolution as a "grave illness,"[19] an eruption that would inevitably disclose the deficiency of creative energy in Russian society. In the summer of 1917, he felt the rising tide of Bolshevism as an irrevocable *fatum*. During the five years he would spend under the Soviet regime, he was exposed to the "moral ugliness" ushered in by the triumph of the Bolshevik cause.[20] A new human type seemed to have appeared in Russia, bearing little similarity to the old revolutionary intelligentsia as he had known it. Instead, these newly emerged men and women manifested some of the repulsive traits of fascist aggressiveness.

In his autobiographical retrospect, Berdyaev interprets the rise of European fascism as the raw response to Lenin's accession to power. His opposition to Bolshevism was spiritual rather than political, but no more absolute than his rejection of what he sees as the lie at the core of bourgeois capitalism, with its debased notion of individualism.

When, in 1922, anti-religious persecution began in earnest, Berdyaev was arrested. During eight days of interrogation, he was brought face to face with Dzerzhinsky, the founder of the Cheka himself. Throughout this ordeal, he remained fearless and explained his convictions frankly and without guile. His demeanor led to his expulsion from the Soviet Union, as a subject adjudged irretrievable for the Revolution. This enforced exit from "the tragi-comedy of History" came as a liberation.[21]

He perceived in it the "accomplishment of my destiny."[22] Nevertheless, the terminal separation from his homeland would weigh heavily on him for the rest of his life.

Berdyaev entered exile with a fully formed philosophical outlook. He would write and publish major new works and see them translated into many languages. These writings established him as an original thinker not only in France, where he lived, but also throughout and beyond Western Europe. But if one thinks of his works as a single whole, one is struck by the coherence and the continuity of his thought. Much of what he wrote in the latter part of his life can be read as a series of brilliant variations on the great themes he brought with him from Russia.

The Meaning of Creativity, which appeared posthumously in French (*Les sens de l'acte créateur, Essai d'une justification de l'homme* [Paris, 1955]), is a case in point. Its original composition dates back to the winter of 1916, part of which Berdyaev spent in Italy. Written in a single blaze of inspiration, this visionary essay illuminates his philosophical conception of the creative act as the locus of a free encounter between the individual human self and the divine. The epigraph inscribes it with the daring thought uttered long ago by the great German mystic Angelus Silesius: "I know, that without me, God could not live an instant." The full power of this paradoxical idea can only be grasped in the riddling, rhymed speech of the German saying: *"Ich weiss, dass ohne mich Gott nicht ein Nu kann leben, Werd' ich zu nicht, er muss von Noth den Geist aufgeben."*[23]

This early intuition, which pushes Christian thought to its limit, animates all of Berdyaev's subsequent meditations about human destiny on this earth. Suspended over the borderline between transcendence and transgression, it contains the essence of *theosis*, a doctrine of human divinization incipient in Eastern Orthodox mysticism. Berdyaev read its imprint in the novels of Dostoevsky and in the arcane writings of his contemporary Nikolai Fedorov, who called on the living to resurrect the dead by the fiat of loving faith. For his part, Berdyaev interpreted the divine need for human co-creation as an urgent summons that historical Christianity had failed to answer. Like Dostoevsky and Vladimir Solovyev before him, he, too, placed this unfinished task in the future.

These metaphysical themes, often interlocked with questions arising from historical actuality or from the realm of Russian culture, would reappear. Berdyaev never stopped meditating on the meaning of his youthful insights. But his restless mind, seeking to recapture his own fully developed thought in the moment of vital comprehension, propelled him to pursue it in a new articulation. All his revisions are rewritings, often with an expanded ambit and a distinctly new context.

The presence of Renaissance Italy, with its art and humanistic culture, is deeply felt in *The Meaning of Creativity*. But the splendor of those achievements is filtered by Berdyaev through the prism of a very Russian anguish, bordering on dissatisfaction. Berdyaev stresses that Russia never knew a Renaissance. That may be why Russians are inclined to see the sphere of culture, and the values of European humanism in particular, as something inherently opposed to the sphere of religion. The urgent appeal of what Ivan Karamazov called the "accursed questions" precludes the patient labor required to build the mansion of a livable human culture. The Petersburg phase of Russian history, which gave birth to a literature that still defines Russian spiritual identity, was haunted by an apocalyptic premonition of its own demise.

Berdyaev understood the meaning of Russian cultural nihilism as the inverted form of its eschatological hope. As for himself, his nimble, deeply cultivated mind was at ease with the great works of European philosophy and literature. His most intimate affinities were with Romanticism, a movement he valued for unleashing a liberating surge of subjectivity. Classicism, with its ideal of symmetry and balance, left him cold. His particular sensibility did not incline him to celebrate the healing art of the Apollonian illusion of objectivity.

A true son of Russia, Berdyaev had a dash of the spirit of Heraclitus in his make-up, inimical to all thought of ontological stasis. In his *Destiny of Man* (1937) he contradicts his beloved master Jakob Boehme, who had located primal freedom, *Ungrund,* within God. For Berdyaev, freedom is uncreated and cannot be derived from being, not even from the divine being of the Pantocrator. He writes: "Out of the Divine Nothing, the *Gottheit* or the *Ungrund,* the Holy Trinity, God the Creator is born. The creation of the world by God the Creator is a secondary act. From this point of view it may be said that freedom is not created by God: it is rooted in the Nothing, in the *Ungrund* for all eternity. Freedom is not determined by God; it is part of the nothing out of which God created the world." In Berdyaev's conception, "Man is the child of freedom—of nothing, of non-being, *to meon.*"[24] He refuses to rationalize this ontological mystery.

Berdyaev's years in France, where he spent most of his exile, only deepened his Russianness. He relished the intellectual stimulation of his exchanges with French thinkers and was an active participant in the meetings at Pontigny.[25] There, in a privileged sanctuary of free thought, he connected with the French existentialist Gabriel Marcel, as well as with other personalities from the literary and academic worlds. The discussions at these conferences ranged from questions of literary and philosophical interest to the problems highlighted by current events and political trends. Berdyaev was charmed by the prevailing atmosphere of civilized informality, but he remained aware of the gap that separated him from his interlocutors. Russian thinkers, he mused, go to the essence of problems, while the French prefer to analyze them in their reflected form, as they appear on the cultural canvas.[26]

Throughout his stay in France, Berdyaev was actively engaged in the intellectual life of the Russian emigré community, centered in Paris. These relations were more intimate but also more painful than his encounters with French intellectuals. As the editor of the philosophical and religious review *Put,'* (a revival of the eponymous journal he had co-founded with Sergei Bulgakov back in 1916 in Russia), he was influential in the movement of Christian youth. He opened the pages of his review to all varieties of opinion and clashed, often bitterly, with the entrenched conservatism of emigré Orthodox clergy.

The thirties, with the rise of Nazism in Germany and the terror of collectivization in the Soviet Union, were a time of dark forebodings. Against this backdrop, the philosophical refuge at Pontigny felt like a fragile vessel floating in stormy waters. With an awareness of these distant threats encroaching on his consciousness, Berdyaev wrote his analysis of contemporary culture in *The Destiny of Man.* Widely admired in Europe from the moment it appeared, this work is now considered a cornerstone of modern philosophical anthropology, equivalent to the pioneering writings of Max Scheler and Ernst Cassirer.

From his early years, Berdyaev's philosophical outlook resonated with the sense of impending endings. But never before did his eschatological vision cast the historical prospects of humanity in such dark hues. In Part II of *The Destiny of Man* ("Morality on this Side of Good and Evil"), he reads the signs of a terminal crisis of Christianity in his explanation of the deadly struggle between the fascist and communist versions of the same spiritual disease. "Liberation of labor is the liberation of personality from the oppressive phantasms of the bourgeois capitalist world," he comments.[27] But he soon adds that if the power of the Communist state takes over from the bourgeoisie the absolute right of property, this "might result in still greater restrictions of freedom."[28] Viewed through his spiritual lens, this is a time when the divine has been emptied out of the human personality. Abandoned by God to the *fatum* of a force of necessity that has no roots in God, humanity has become the tool of a power-drive which knows no meaning beyond itself.

The Origin of Russian Communism (1937), which confirmed Berdyaev's status as a cultural historian, emerged out of the same time-frame. But to this reader it seems gentler in its treatment of the modern human condition. It is as if a retrospective analysis of the ways of the Russian intelligentsia had brought him back in sympathy with the hopes of liberation he once shared with them. Paradoxically, Berdyaev, who lectured on Dostoevsky under the Soviet rule, now draws attention to the spiritual impetus within Bolshevism.

Berdyaev survived World War II and continued writing in Clamart, where he had retreated from Paris. His reputation was at its height when he died, at the threshold of the Cold War. His works, many of which appeared posthumously in English, spread his European fame into North America.[29] He is remembered as an existentialist philosopher and an original interpreter of Russian thought. But after the collapse of Communism, with religion resurgent in all societies, it is his vision of humano-divinity that speaks most urgently to what ails us. Too often, religious expression looks backward, deriving authority from rituals that celebrate the divisive aggression of ethnicity. Berdyaev tells us that the failed *apotheosis* of the secular man calls for the supremely creative venture of *theosis,* a mystical process through which the human self meets the divine without disappearing in it.

Maria Nemcova Banerjee

NOTES

1. *Samopoznanie, Opyt filosofskoi avtobiografii* (Paris, 1949). I quote from the introduction, dated 1940, p. 8. All the translations from this text are mine. The autobiography is available in English translation, under the title, *Nikolai Berdyaev, Dream and Reality,* trans. by Katharine Lampert (New York, 1951).
2. Samopoznanie, ch. I, 13.
3. Ibid., ch. VII, 218.
4. *Landmarks, A Collection of Essays on the Russian Intelligentsia, 1909* (Berdyaev, Bulgakov, Gershenzon, Izgoev, Kistiakovsky, Struve, Frank), trans. by Marian Schwartz (New York, 1977). "Philosophic Truth and the Moral Truth of the Intelligentsia," by Nikolai Berdyaev, 3-22.
5. Ibid., 4.
6. Ibid., 22.
7. *Dostoevsky,* trans. by Donald Attwater (New York, 1956), ch. VIII, "The Grand Inquisitor. Christ and Antichrist," 188.
8. *Samopoznanie,* ch. IX, 253-258.
9. *Dostoevsky,* ch. VIII, 188.
10. Ibid., ch. III, "Freedom," 67.
11. Ibid., 71.
12. Ibid., 69.
13. Ibid., 70.
14. Ibid., 70.
15. Ibid., 70.
16. *The Brothers Karamazov,* ed. Ralph Matlaw (New York, 1976), part II, book 5, "Pro and Contra," ch. V, "The Grand Inquisitor," 243.
17. *Dostoevsky,* ch. III, 87.
18. *Samopoznanie,* ch. VII, 190.
19. Ibid., ch. IX, 245.
20. Ibid., 248.

21. Ibid., 267.
22. Ibid., 264.
23. *Smysl tvorchestva, Opyt opravdaniia cheloveka*, 2nd ed., (Paris, 1985), in vol. 2 of *Sobranie sochinenii Nikolaia Berdyaeva*.
24. *The Destiny of Man*, trans. by Natalie Duddington (London, 1937), Part I "Principles," ch. 2, "Origin of Good and Evil," 25.
25. *Samopoznanie*, ch. X, 268-309.
26. Ibid., 275.
27. *The Destiny of Man*, part II, ch. 4, "Concrete Problems of Ethics," 216.
28. Ibid., 218.
29. N. O. Lossky, in *History of Russian Philosophy*, under the rubrique "N. Berdyaev," gives a good bibliography of Berdyaev's philosophical works. For a list of works Berdyaev wrote in France, see *Samopoznanie*, ch. XI, "Ma philosophie definitive. Profession de foi. Le monde eschatologique. Temps et éternité," 362.

FOREWORD

Russian nineteenth-century thought was mainly preoccupied with problems of the philosophy of history which, indeed, laid the foundations of our national consciousness. It is no accident that our spiritual interests were centred upon the disputes of the slavophiles and westerners about Russia and Europe, the East and West. Chaadayev and the slavophiles had helped to turn Russian speculation towards these problems, for, to them, the enigma of Russia and of her historical destiny was synonymous with that of the philosophy of history. Thus the elaboration of a religious philosophy of history would appear to be the specific mission of Russian philosophical thought, which has always had a predilection for the eschatological problem and apocalypticism. This is what distinguishes it from Western thought and also gives it a religious character.

I have personally always been particularly engrossed in these problems. The World War and the Russian Revolution only served to stimulate my interest and to concentrate my researches pre-eminently in this field. I finally planned a book treating of the fundamental problems of the philosophy of history, and I used this plan as the basis for a series of lectures delivered in Moscow at the Liberal Academy of Spiritual Culture in 1919-1920. These notes are incorporated in the present volume. To them I have, however, appended an article, 'The Will to Life and to Culture', which I wrote in 1922 and which constitutes an essential element of my conception of the philosophy of history.

NICOLAS BERDYAEV

[xxv]

TRANSLATOR'S NOTE

In an age only comparable with the Hellenistic for its diversity of opinion, its easy acceptance of pseudo-faiths and its glib rationalistic exposition of the sacred mysteries, it is above all necessary to seek an antidote to the disintegration of the human personality implied in these processes. The exteriorization of human energies since the Renaissance, the transformation of the Gothic Cathedral, that dynamic but harmonious spiritual edifice, into a superficially expanded realm linked by the mechanical necessity of steam-boat, locomotive and air-plane, has naturally tended to discredit man's deeper, organic aspirations. Hence the complete spiritual disorientation of modern life and civilization only too evident in the arts and literature, the faithful mirrors of their time.

To grasp and oppose the complex phenomenon of social and cultural disintegration, we must rely upon the criterion of some integral dialectic. The moment has come, indeed, when we should attempt, on the basis of fundamental principles, to *integrate* our historical experience in a Europe which, though torn by schism, can still claim to be the descendant of Christendom. The elements of such a dialectic are present in Spengler. Professor Berdyaev's approach, however, is more deeply religious, and his dialectic is inseparable from a dynamic and integral interpretation of Christianity, which, he affirms, is based essentially upon the freedom of good and evil, that is, upon an antithesis giving it a tragic and dynamic character absent from the pre-Christian and non-Christian worlds. This explains, too, the interior dialogue underlying Western literature from St. Augustine to Dostoievsky, Proust, Joyce, and even a section of Soviet writers.

The Meaning of History, paradoxically enough, was projected and first delivered as a series of lectures in Soviet Russia, from which Professor Berdyaev was later expelled. These lectures are now reproduced in their original form. That explains why certain social phenomena like Fascism are not dealt with in greater detail, and why Professor Berdyaev stops with Futurism as the latest manifestation of European art. This fact, however, in no way detracts from the original value of *The Meaning of History*, which is essentially an exposition of the general principles of a Christian dialectic. Recent history, indeed, has tended to confirm rather than disprove Professor Berdyaev's prophecies and prognostications. In any case, the value and possibilities of such a dialectic become increasingly apparent in a world which is threatening to revert to a Hobbesian state of nature.

G. R.

CHAPTER I

ON THE ESSENCE OF THE HISTORICAL:
THE MEANING OF TRADITION

Catastrophic moments in world history have always proved an incitement to speculation. They have stimulated attempts to define the historical process and to build up this or that philosophy of history. It has been so always. St. Augustine's was the first notable philosophy of history. It was worked out during the early Christian period and determined to a large extent the elaboration of future philosophies of history. Moreover, it coincided with one of the most catastrophic moments of world history—the collapse of the ancient world and the fall of Rome. The Book of Daniel represented the first attempt to establish a philosophy of history in the pre-Christian world; and it had likewise been exclusively concerned with the catastrophic events in the destiny of the Jewish people. Again, after the great French Revolution and the Napoleonic wars, the human mind turned towards constructive thought in the sphere of the philosophy of history and sought to grasp and define the historical process. Thus the philosophy of history plays an important part in the conceptions of J. de Maistre and Bonald.

There can be little doubt, I think, that not only Russia but Europe and the world as a whole are now entering upon a catastrophic period of their development. We are living at a time of immense crisis, on the threshold of a new era. The very structure of historical development has suffered a profound change. It is now essentially different from what it was prior to the World War and the Russian and the European Revolutions.

This change can only be regarded as catastrophic. Volcanic sources have opened in the historical substrata. Everything is tottering, and we have the impression of a particularly intense and acute movement of historical forces. An important result of this has been to sharpen man's awareness, to direct his thought and conscience to the examination and revaluation of the fundamental problems and to the elaboration of a new philosophy of history. We are entering upon an era in which man's consciousness will be more than ever concerned with these problems. It is precisely to them that I should like to devote my attention. But before venturing to deal with the very essence of the fundamental problems of the philosophy of history, or, more exactly, the metaphysics of history, I shall have to make a digression on the essential nature of the 'historical'.

What do we understand by the 'historical'? To comprehend and define it, one must, to begin with, have experienced a certain spiritual dismemberment. In periods when the human spirit has been wholly and organically contained in some fully crystallized, fully matured and settled epoch, the problems of philosophy, of historical movement and of the meaning of history, do not arise with the same urgency. This type of organic epoch does not favour either historical awareness or the elaboration of a philosophy of history. Before the historical object and subject can be opposed it is necessary for a disruption to have occurred in man's historical life and conscience. He must also have developed the faculty of speculation without which there can exist no possibility either of historical science or of an elaboration of a philosophy of history.

In view of this, we may establish three periods in relation to the historical. Firstly, a period that is one of direct integral and organic experience in some settled historical order. A period of this kind is, of course, of great interest to historical science, but the latter has as yet no function within it. Here thought is static; and that explains why the dynamism of the object of historical science is not yet clearly grasped by the human mind.

Secondly, there is the period of fateful and menacing schism and disruption, when the foundations of an established order are tottering. It is in this collapse of organic structure and vital rhythm that the historical process originates, with its train of catastrophes and calamities of varying intensity. The result of this schism and disruption is that the knowing subject no longer feels himself directly and wholly a part of the historical object; and this gives birth to the speculations of historical science. But this does not favour either a real elaboration of a philosophy of history or a real definition of the historical process, because it involves a divorce between subject and object, and the withdrawal of the speculating subject from the life in which he had hitherto directly participated. He is separated from the innermost life, from the 'historical' itself. An antithesis is set up between the 'historical' and the knowing subject, now divorced from the inner essence of the former. This period sees the development of historical science and may even give rise to an historical point of view, that is, to a general interpretation of culture.

But there exists—and this is one of the paradoxes upon which we shall dwell—between the 'historical' itself, on the one hand, and such an awareness of history, on the other, not so much an affinity as a sharp distinction and even a contradiction. Such an awareness of history, although it may have certain affinities with historical science, is yet very far removed from the mysterious nature of the 'historical'. Not only does it not approach this mystery, but it would seem to have lost all means of communication with it. Not only does it not help to apprehend and understand the nature of the 'historical', it even denies its existence. In order for man to commune with the inner mystery of the 'historical', in which he participates directly in organic and co-ordinated periods of human life without being intellectually aware of or speculating upon it, he must have experienced the antithesis of the knowing subject and the object known. And after experiencing the mysteries of schism he will again commune with the mystery of the 'historical'. In order to define the historical process and build up a real philosophy of history he will have to rediscover the mysterious sources of historical life, its inner significance and the inner soul of history.

Thirdly, there is the period that implies a return to the 'historical'. Thus, when I say that catastrophic moments are particularly propitious for the elaboration of a philosophy of history, I have in view those catastrophes when the human spirit, having experienced the collapse of a given historical order and the moment of schism and disintegration, is able to appose and oppose these two moments—that of the direct participation in an historical order and that of the divorce from it—in order to arrive at a third spiritual state which induces a particularly acute consciousness, a particular aptitude for speculation and a corresponding aspiration towards the mysteries of the 'historical'. Such a state is especially favourable to the consideration of the problems of the philosophy of history. But to make clear what I mean by my assertion that the second period, that of disintegration and speculation, in which historical science has its rise and in which the attempt is made to build up a philosophy of history, is always fatally wanting in depth and in penetration into the mysteries of history, I propose to review briefly the characteristics of that epoch of human culture generally known as 'the age of enlightenment'.

By the 'age of enlightenment' or the *Aufklärung* I do not intend simply to designate the eighteenth century, which was the classical period of enlightenment in modern history. I believe that the cultures of all times and of all peoples have passed through a period of enlightenment. The cultural development of all peoples is subject to a certain cyclic movement. This affinity between cultural processes would seem to indicate the organic character of their development. Thus, Greek culture, one of the greatest known to mankind, had its age of enlightenment essentially analogous to that experienced by mankind in the eighteenth century. The age of the sophists was in its way the flowering of Greek culture; but in spite of its specifically Hellenic features it had many particularities in common with the age of eighteenth century enlightenment. As the eighteenth century enlightenment was to do, and as every age of enlightenment tends to do, the age of Greek enlightenment attacked and discredited what was sacred in the 'historical' and all the organic and traditional elements of history.

An age of enlightenment is that age in the history of every

people when the self-confident human reason rears itself above the mysteries of being and of life, above those divine mysteries which are the source of all human life and culture. In such an age the human reason places itself outside and above these immediate mysteries of life. It is characterized by the attempt to appoint limited human reason as judge of the mysteries of universal creation and history. It follows inevitably that man ceases to participate directly in the 'historical'. The age of enlightenment denies the mystery of the 'historical'. It denies the 'historical' all specific reality and contact with the human spirit and the human reason.

Thus the age of eighteenth-century enlightenment was profoundly anti-historical, in spite of the fact that Voltaire was the first to use the term 'philosophy of history' and of the publication of a whole series of historical works and treatises. It has become an axiom that it was thanks to the Romantic revival, to the reaction directed at the beginning of the nineteenth century against the enlightenment of the eighteenth, that we were enabled to apprehend the mystery of the 'historical' and study it seriously. It was thanks to this spiritual reaction that we recovered the myths and traditions of historical antiquity which the age of enlightenment had sought to discredit. True, the latter had made attempts to grasp and define them, but it had of course done so in its own fashion.

The enlightened reason of the eighteenth and nineteenth centuries was a self-assertive and limited reason. It was not in communion with the reason of universal history; for there exists, indeed, an historical reason from which this enlightened reason was breaking away and over which it was setting itself up as judge. Enlightened reason claimed to be the judge of the organic reason of history; but in reality a higher reason ought to transcend the mere rational consciousness peculiar to a given organic epoch, that, let us say, of the eighteenth and nineteenth centuries with all their insufficiencies and defects. Reason ought to be attuned to the primal wisdom of man, to those first apprehensions of being and of life which are born with the dawn of human history or even prehistory, and to that animistic conception of life which is common to all peoples in the earliest stages of their existence. This wisdom which is shared by the very earliest epochs persists in the inner mysterious depths of life throughout the history of the human spirit, the birth of Christianity and the Middle Ages, down to our times. Only a reason based upon such wisdom can claim to be the true illuminating and enlightened reason. But that 'enlightened' reason which celebrated its classical triumphs in the eighteenth century knew comparatively little; its sympathies were few, its intelligence limited, and it had lost all inner contact with the mysteries of the historical life. This blindness of the 'enlightened' reason was the inner penalty it paid for its self-assertiveness and for the egoism with which it enslaved both the human and the superhuman.

On the other hand, the triumph of the enlightened reason gave birth to that science which opposed the knowing subject to the known object of history; and in this sphere it accomplished a great deal. It succeeded in relating, collecting, amassing and partially apprehending very much. But its activities were accompanied by a deep impotence to grasp the very essence of the 'historical'. The known object itself gradually recedes, is lost sight of and ceases to exist as that primal reality which constitutes its only claim to be called historical and its only means of revealing the sources of history. This process is particularly flagrant in the sphere of historical criticism. Historical science became possible only in the nineteenth century. In the preceding century it had been considered possible to assert, for example, that religion had been invented by priests in order to deceive the people. But such an assertion becomes impossible in the nineteenth century.

The above process can be seen most clearly at work in the sphere of ecclesiastical history. This was a new sphere which had formerly been forbidden ground. It is of interest therefore to examine the nature of the critical work taking place in it. In the Christian world everything is based upon the sacred tradition and upon its acceptance. But historical criticism set out to discredit this tradition. It had begun to do so already in the age of the Reformation, which was the first to doubt the sacred tradition. The work of discrediting it was developed until it led ultimately to the discrediting of the Scriptures themselves, which were in reality an inalienable part of the sacred tradition. Therefore the denial of the sacred tradition involves that of the Scriptures in their turn.

I give this example to illustrate the fact that historical criticism had become absolutely powerless to explain the mystery of the religious phenomenon. It hovered around this mystery; but it could not solve that of the origins of Christianity. The whole of the voluminous German critical literature in this sphere, though it has done undoubted service in the working out of all sorts of material, confesses its impotence to resolve this mystery. There seems to be no grasp or vision of the essentials. Some fundamental mystery which had formed an inalienable part of tradition now disappears leaving only the husk of history. This critical tendency may likewise be observed in the sphere of history in general. History and culture also possess a sacred tradition; and it is only when the knowing subject has not broken away from the inner life that he can feel himself to be in communion with it. But once he has become divorced from it, he must pursue the path of self-denial to the bitter end. The result is the wholesale unmasking of historical mysteries and history becomes reduced to a mere ghost of itself.

The great contribution of Marx's economic materialism, which is one of the most interesting currents in the philosophy of history, consists in its having asserted the ultimate consequences of that rationalization of the historical mysteries and traditions which, in historical science, dates from the age of enlightenment. The Marxist interpretation of history is the only one that logically, consistently and uncompromisingly analyses and discredits historical mysteries and traditions. The impugnment of the mystery of the 'historical' in the sphere of religion, initiated at the Reformation, became more general in the age of enlightenment and reached its full development as a fundamental principle of historical science in the nineteenth century. But it had only gone half way. Most of the ideological currents of historical science failed to complete the task of discrediting the historical. Some shreds of it still remained. Only economic materialism, because it questioned all tradition and all the sacred associations of history, pursued this task to the very end and accomplished an act of rebellion against the 'historical'. As interpreted by economic materialism the historical process appears devoid of soul. Everything is stripped of soul, of inner and mysterious life. The impugnment of the divine mysteries elicits the process of materialistic economic production as the only reality of the historical process and the economic forms that are born of the former as the only ontological, primal and real ones. Everything else appears to be secondary, contingent and superficial. Religion, spirituality, culture, art, human life itself, all are presented as the merest accidents of matter in movement and devoid of substantial reality.

Thus is accomplished the final process of the de-animation of history and the annihilation of its inner mysteries. This is effected through the exposure of the chief mystery, its reduction by historical materialism to terms of production and the development of mankind's productive forces. Thus culminates the critical work of destruction which had its origin in the age of enlightenment, but which repudiated the idea of 'enlightenment' itself. Marx's economic materialism dethrones the idea of 'enlightenment' in its eighteenth-century rationalistic form and substitutes for it an original type of evolutionism. It also demonstrates that the latest developments of 'enlightenment' do not lead anywhere, least of all to a solution of the mystery of the inner destiny of peoples, of their spiritual life, or of mankind as a whole. Instead, therefore, of considering these problems, economic materialism denies them as illusory and as the product purely of given economic conditions. But economic materialism reveals a fundamental contradiction which it is unable to resolve because it cannot rise superior to it. And this contradiction is patent to any one who is prepared to submit the materialist doctrine to a trial in the court of philosophy.

For if economic materialism really contends that the human consciousness is no more than an adjunct of man's economic activities, then how are we to explain the origin of the intellect manifested by the prophets of economic materialism themselves, of that manifested by Marx and Engels, which towers above the mere passive reflection of economic relations? When founding his doctrine, Marx claimed to possess that type of reason which transcends the purely passive reflex of economic activities. But if the ideological structure of economic materialism represents no more than the figment of given productive relations, of those, let us say, which came into being in the nineteenth century as a result of the struggle of the proletariat against the bourgeoisie, then it is incomprehensible how the prophets of this doctrine can claim to possess a greater measure of truth than all those others whose systems are qualified as a self-delusion born of this very figment. In that case their doctrine is but another illusion generated by the same economic reality.

Thus Marxism has worked out the pretensions and presumptions of 'enlightened reason' to its ultimate conclusion. It believes itself to be the possessor of that enlightened and illuminating reason which transcends the universal and historical destiny of mankind, as well as its entire spiritual life and all the human ideologies; and it claims to expose their delusions and illusions, which in reality are, like itself, no more than a reflex of the economic process. By its claim to be the unique 'light-bearing' consciousness—one that is no mere ideology, but the unique and ultimate revelation of the mystery of the historical process—Marxism represents a striving to unite the pretensions of enlightened reason with claims comparable with those of ancient Israel.

In fact, what it does succeed in revealing is not so much the mystery of the historical process as its external manifestations, the terrifying void of the historical destiny of mankind, the distressing abyss of human history and the non-existence of the human spirit in all its manifestations, religion, philosophy, invention, science and art. This repudiation of the spirit constitutes the strength and originality of Marxism. I believe the negative contribution of such a system to be very great. Firstly, it helps to destroy all the half-digested and semi-ideological currents which had formed themselves in the nineteenth and twentieth centuries. Secondly, it poses the dilemma either of adapting oneself to this mystery of non-existence and of plunging into its abyss, or of communing once again with the imponderable mystery of the inner destiny, of the inner traditions and mysteries; a communion that has suffered and overcome the ordeal of a triple iconoclasm, destructive, critical and negative.

Historical science and the philosophy of history, like every sphere of human knowledge, ought to possess their own gnosiology and their own theory of knowledge. What I have said so far refers more particularly to this sphere, whose ultimate goal is the apprehension of the nature of the 'historical' as a certain specific reality existing in the hierarchy of realities which compose being. This historical knowledge has as its goal an absolutely specific and original object which cannot be sub-divided into other objects either material or spiritual. It is, of course, impossible to regard the 'historical' as a reality of a material, physiological or geographical order. It is likewise unthinkable to consider historical reality in erms of any psychic reality. The 'historical' has its peculiar and specific nature; it is a reality of a particular kind, a particular stage of existence. The acceptance of historical tradition and of communion with history is indispensable for the knowledge of what constitutes the specifically 'historical'. Historical speculation is impossible outside the category of historical tradition. The acceptance of this latter forms a certain *a priori*, a certain absolute category for all historical knowledge. Outside of it one finds very few avenues of approach to the problem.

The process to which historical materialism submits history leads inevitably to the crumbling away of historical reality. The latter is above all a concrete and not an abstract reality; and no concrete reality other than the historical does or can exist. The 'historical' is essentially a coherent form of existence. For the concrete in its literal sense signifies something that grows together and coheres, as opposed to the abstract, detached, dissociated and divided. Everything abstract is by its nature opposed to the historical. Sociology has to do with what is detached and abstract, while history deals only with the concrete. The former treats of conceptions such as those of class and the social group which are all abstract categories. The social group or class is merely an intellectual superstructure devoid of substantial existence. The 'historical', on the other hand, is an object of an altogether different order; it is both concrete and particular while sociology is both abstract and general. The latter does not deal with any particular conceptions; the former deals with nothing else. Everything genuinely historical has both a particular and a concrete character. Carlyle, the most concrete and particular of the historians, says that John Lackland came upon this earth on such and such a day. This indeed is the very substance of history.

An attempt has been made to elaborate a philosophy of history on the basis of the principles of Kantian philosophy.

Its exponent was Rikkert, of the Windelband School, who argued that historical knowledge differed from that of the natural sciences as conceptions of the particular from those of the general. This contention, as presented by Rikkert, appears rather one-sided; but it has the merit of drawing attention to the fact that we have to deal with the concrete and the particular in the sphere of history. Rikkert's presentation of the problem, however, is false, because there are cases in which the general may itself be the particular. As an illustration of this let us take the term 'historical nation'. This latter is a general concept; but a concrete historical nation is at the same time an absolutely historical concept. The age-long dispute between the Nominalists and the Realists reveals an insufficient grasp of the mystery of the particular. Nor had the particular been revealed to Plato. The apprehension of being as a gradation of particularities does not necessarily imply Nominalism, for the general can also be the particular.

In view of my future argument it is most important to establish the opposition between the historical and the sociological. My book is concerned not with the problems of sociology but with those of the philosophy and the knowledge of historical destinies. The philosophy of history—of historical knowledge—is one of the ways to the knowledge of spiritual reality. It is a science of the spirit bringing us into communion with the mysteries of spiritual life. It deals with that concrete spiritual reality, so much richer and more complex than that revealed, for example, in individual human psychology. The philosophy of history studies man in the concrete fulness of his spiritual being; psychology, physiology and the other spheres of human knowledge study him incompletely in one or other of his aspects. The philosophy of history examines man in relation to the world forces which act upon him, that is, in his greatest fulness and concreteness. By comparison all other ways of approaching man are abstract.

Human destiny can be grasped only through this concrete knowledge of the philosophy of history. Other sciences do not set out to study the human destiny, which is a complex of the actions of all the world forces. This complex of world forces gives rise to that reality of a higher and special order which we term historical reality. Thus, although material forces and economic factors do play an important part in history, and although historical materialism, which I spiritually repudiate, cannot be denied a partial truth, yet the material factor operating in historical reality is itself based upon a deeper spiritual foundation. It must in fact be ultimately considered as a spiritual force. Material elements are only part of spiritual historical reality. The whole of man's economic life, indeed, reposes upon a spiritual foundation. We shall have to dwell upon this fact again when considering the various problems of the philosophy of history.

Man is in the highest degree an historical being. He is situated in history and history is situated in him. Between man and history there exists such a deep, mysterious, primordial and coherent relationship, such a concrete interdependence, that a divorce between them is impossible. It is as impossible to detach man from history and to consider him abstractly as it is to detach history from man and to examine it from without, that is, from a non-human point of view. Nor is it possible to consider man isolated from the profoundest spiritual reality of history. The 'historical' cannot be regarded, as

[15]

the various philosophical schools have tended to regard it, as a mere phenomenon, as a manifestation of the outer world offered to our experience; and it cannot be opposed, as Kant opposed it, to the noumenal reality, to the very essence of the inner occult reality. I believe that history and the 'historical' are not merely phenomena, that they are—and this is the most radical hypothesis of the philosophy of history—noumena. The historical in the real sense of the word brings with it the revelation of essential being, of the inner spiritual nature of the world and of the inner spiritual essence of man, and not merely of the external phenomena. The 'historical' is by its nature not phenomenal but deeply ontological. It has its roots in some deep primal foundation of being which it makes available for our communion and understanding. The 'historical' is a sort of revelation of the deepest essence of universal reality, of the destiny of the world focused in that of man. It is a revelation of noumenal reality. The noumenal 'historical' can be approached only through the most intimate concrete tie between man and history, between the destiny of the former and the metaphysics of historical forces.

In order to grasp the mystery of the 'historical', I must have a sense of it and history as something that is deeply *mine*, that is deeply *my* history, that is deeply *my* destiny. I must situate myself within historical destiny and it within my own human destiny. The presence of the historical destiny then becomes revealed in the very depths of the human spirit. All historical epochs, from the very earliest to that at the topmost peak of modern history, represent my historical destiny; they are all mine.

This approach is diametrically opposed to that which

[16]

favours the work of destructive criticism as applied to the historical process. The latter only serves to divorce man, the human spirit and history from each other, making them mutually incomprehensible, hostile and alien. The way we have chosen leads backwards; for we must not approach the historical process as something that is alien to us, that is imposed upon us, that crushes and enslaves us, and against which we rebel both in our knowledge and action. Such a course would only lead us to the brink of a gaping void and abyss which lie concealed in both history and man himself. But the approach, which I would advocate and which alone can help us to build up a real philosophy of history, consists in a profound integration of my historical destiny with that of mankind which is so intimately related to me. In the destiny of mankind I must recognize my own destiny, and in the latter that of history. This is the only way in which we can commune with the mystery of the 'historical' and discover in it the great spiritual destinies of mankind. And, inversely, this is the only way in which we can realize all the riches and values in our possession and unite our own individual destiny with that of universal history instead of merely discovering the void of our isolation in opposition to all the riches of universal historical life. Thus the real goal of the philosophy of history is to establish a bond between man and history, between man's destiny and the metaphysics of history.

History, since it is synonymous with the greatest spiritual reality, is not a given empirical fact or a naked factual material. As such it neither exists nor can be apprehended. It can, however, be approached through the historical memory, that is, through a certain spiritual activity, a certain given

[17]

spiritual relation to the 'historical' within the sphere of historical knowledge which, as a result, becomes inwardly transfigured and transformed. The inner soul of history emerges in all its clarity only in the process of transformation and transfiguration which takes place in historical memory. This is as true for the apprehension of the soul of history as it is for that of man: for the human personality, when not bound by memory into an integral whole, lacks the faculty of apprehending the human soul as a certain reality. But the historical memory as a means of knowing the 'historical' is inalienably part of the historical tradition outside of which it has no existence. The abstract use of documents never leads to the knowledge of the 'historical'. It does not bring us into communion with the latter. Moreover, however necessary and important the study of historical monuments may be, it is meaningless when undertaken without reference to the historical tradition with which historical memory is associated. The latter only undoes the knot that binds man's spiritual destiny to that of history. No great cultural epoch, whether that of Hellenic culture or that of the birth of Christianity, that of the flowering of the Middle Ages or that of the Renaissance, is comprehensible unless we approach it through the historical memory, whose data constitute our spiritual past, our spiritual culture and our ultimate source. To grasp these great epochs we must inform them with our own spiritual destiny, for, considered superficially, they are all inwardly dead to us. But the historical memory, which obliges us to commune inwardly with the 'historical', is an inalienable part of the historical tradition.

The historical tradition is precisely this inner historical memory which is transposed into historical destiny. The philosophy of history represents a certain spiritualization and transfiguration of the historical process. In a certain sense, historical memory implies a merciless war between eternity and time; and the philosophy of history is always the witness of the triumph of eternity over time and corruption. It signifies the triumph of the incorruptible. It is a monument to the victory of the spirit of incorruptibility over that of corruptibility. The goal of historical knowledge and philosophy is not natural but supernatural. For just as there exists an after-life in relation to individual life, so the great historical paths likewise lead us to such a world. And that explains why the historical memory, when directed to contemplating the past, evokes an absolutely peculiar feeling of communion with a world other than the empirical, whose nightmare oppression we must overcome before we can attain to that historical reality which is the authentic revelation of other worlds.

The philosophy of history is therefore that of an after-world rather than that of empirical realities. When wandering in the Roman Campagna, where occurred the mysterious blending of the after-world with the historical world, where historical monuments became the manifestations of nature, we commune with another sort of life, with the mysteries of the past, with those of the after-world; we commune with the mysteries in which eternity is triumphant over corruption and death. Thus the real philosophy of history is that of the triumph of authentic life over death; it is the communion of man with another everlastingly broader and richer reality than that in which he is empirically immersed. How pitiful, empty and transient would be the whole of human content if there existed for the individual man no means of communing with the experience of history! In his daily life man has glimpses of the true reality of the great historical world, not only when he is occupied with the building up of a philosophy of history (he is but rarely concerned with this!), but also in many of the spiritual acts of his life. For this he has to thank the historical memory, his inner tradition, the inner communion of the destinies of his individual spirit with those of history. Thus he communes with an everlastingly richer reality, triumphing ultimately over his corruptibility and pettiness, and transcending his poor and limited vision.

CHAPTER II

ON THE NATURE OF THE HISTORICAL: THE METAPHYSICAL AND THE HISTORICAL

History is not an objective empirical datum; it is a myth. Myth is no fiction, but a reality; it is, however, one of a different order from that of the so-called objective empirical fact. Myth is the story preserved in popular memory of a past event and transcends the limits of the external objective world, revealing an ideal world, a subject-object world of facts. According to Schelling, mythology is the primordial history of mankind. But myths are not peculiar to the remote past; various more recent epochs have been rich in the elements of myth-creation.

All great historical epochs, even those of modern history with their tendency to discredit mythology, give rise to myths. Thus the age of the great French Revolution, although ushered in by the rationalistic enlightenment, teems with myths. In the first place there is the myth of the Revolution itself, which was fostered by historians for a long enough period of time; it was only much later that they began to discredit it, as Taine had done in his *History of the Revolution*. Similar myths were current concerning the age of the Renaissance and the Reformation, the Middle Ages, not to speak of remoter periods of history when thought had not as yet been illuminated by the bright light of reason.

A purely objective history would be incomprehensible. We seek an inner profound and mysterious tie with the historical object. It is necessary for both the subject and the object to be historical: the subject of historical knowledge should sense and discover what is essentially historical within himself. And it is in proportion to the discovery of the 'historical' within himself that the subject apprehends the great periods of history. Without a tie of this sort, without this personal inner sense of his participation in the 'historical', he —the subject—could not apprehend history. History demands faith: it is no mere coercion of the knowing subject by external objective facts; it is rather an act transfiguring the great historical past, an act ministering the apperception of the historical object and its essential union with the subject. Their divorce, on the other hand, would make such a comprehension impossible. This has convinced me that historical science ought to adapt to its needs, with certain modifications it is true, the Platonic doctrine of knowledge as an act of remembrance. For any penetration into a great historical epoch is fruitful and based upon real knowledge only when there occurs an act of remembrance. An act of this sort evokes all the past greatness of mankind, a sense of profound association and identification between the innermost experience of the knowing subject and its various historical correlatives.

Each man represents by virtue of his inner nature a sort of microcosm in which the whole world of reality and all the great historical epochs combine and coexist. He is not merely a minute fragment of the universe, but rather a world in his own right, a world revealed or hidden according as consciousness is more or less penetrating and extensive. In this development of self-consciousness the whole history of the world is apprehended, together with all the great epochs which historical science investigates, by submitting them to the critical test of historical monuments, scriptures and archaeological data. But assuming an external stimulus for every profound act of remembrance, it should be possible for man to apprehend history within himself; he should be able, for example, to discover within himself the profoundest strata of the Hellenic world and thus grasp the essentials of Greek history. Similarly, the historian must discover within himself the deep strata of Jewish history before he can grasp its essential nature.

Thus this microcosm would seem to contain in itself all the historical epochs of the past which have not been entirely covered over by the subsequent strata of time and of more recent historical life; these past epochs may appear to be buried in the depths, but they can never be completely obliterated. The inner clarification and elaboration of man's consciousness ought therefore to help him to burst through the outer strata and penetrate into the depths of time, a penetration that is really into the depths of his own nature. Only deep down in his own self can man really discover the secrets of time; for these, far from being something superficial and alien, something imposed and forced upon him from without, represent on the contrary the deepest and most mysterious strata implicit in himself. A narrow consciousness would either disregard these strata or relegate them to a secondary plane.

Historical myths have a profound significance for the act of remembrance. A myth contains the story that is preserved in popular memory and that helps to bring to life some deep

[23]

stratum buried in the depths of the human spirit. The divorce of the subject from object as the result of enlightened criticism may provide material for historical knowledge; but in so far as it destroys the myth and dissociates the depths of time from those of man, it only serves to divorce man from history. It also leads us to reconsider the significance of the part played by tradition in the inner comprehension of history. For the historical tradition which criticism had thought to discredit makes possible a great and occult act of remembrance. It represents, indeed, no external impulse or externally imposed fact alien to man, but one that is a manifestation of the inner mysterious life, in which he can attain to the knowledge of himself and feel himself to be an inalienable participant.

I do not mean to imply that tradition should be exempt from historical criticism or accepted at its own valuation or taken for granted without question. I believe that historical criticism has done a great deal of objective and scientific work in this sphere, and that there exists no justification for re-establishing a merely traditional history. My argument is rather that tradition possesses an inner value. This latter, however, must not be made to depend upon fables such as that, for example, of the foundation of Rome, which was discredited by Niebuhr and the more recent historians. The tradition of a people is valuable in so far as it symbolizes the historical destiny of that people. This symbolism is of primary importance for the elaboration of a philosophy of history and for the apprehension of its inner significance. Tradition is synonymous with the knowledge of historical life; for its symbolism reveals the inner life and the profound organic union of historical reality with that which man discovers through his own spiritual self-knowledge. This tie between tradition and the revelations of self-knowledge is in the highest degree precious. The external facts of history have a tremendous importance. But the inner current of mysterious life, whose flow even external reality cannot intercept, is much more important for the building up of a philosophy of history. It proves that history is to be apprehended only from within and that this apprehension depends more and more on the inner state of our consciousness, on its breadth and depth.

But historical criticism and science postulate as the only true state of consciousness and self-knowledge one that is very narrow and superficial. In this lies its aberration. Much that appears to be objective, irrefutable and convincing in this criticism is only so to the primary and superficial layer of consciousness. But a profounder approach reveals that this is not that true consciousness which is to be found only within historical reality. When we read a history text-book, we are bound to feel that the history and culture of ancient peoples have been utterly emptied of soul and all inner life, leaving nothing but a sort of superficial photograph or sketch. We may therefore be entitled to conclude that the so-called 'historical' criticism is but a transient stage in the historical development through which man's knowledge has to pass. It is one of those transient stages that are least real and profound, and are merely a prelude to man's emergence into an entirely different era with a new sense of responsibility towards the historical process. Then and only then will this inner tradition, this inner myth of history, which had been discredited in the period of historical criticism, transform and define itself anew.

As I have insisted from the beginning, the destiny of man's life on earth is the theme of history. But man's destiny, which fulfils itself in the history of peoples, is first apprehended as such in the spirit of the knowing subject. The history of the world and that of mankind are fulfilled not only in the object and, objectively, in the macrocosm, but also in the microcosm. The connection between these two fulfilments is essential to the metaphysics of history and implies a special relation between the historical and the metaphysical. The opposition between these latter had long been the dominant conception in science and philosophy as well as in certain forms of the religious consciousness, the Hindoo, for example. It is based on the assumption that the metaphysical cannot manifest itself in the historical; and it did not consider the possibility of the historical being other than a merely external and empirical fact which, methodologically, must always be antithetical to everything metaphysical.

Another point of view holds that the metaphysical may be transposed and made manifest in terms of the historical. This standpoint is particularly favourable to the elaboration of a philosophy of history, postulating as it does a sort of historical centre where the metaphysical and the historical meet. But, as I shall attempt to prove, the metaphysical and the historical are really brought together and intimately fused only in the Christian philosophy of history. The conception, too, of tradition as the profoundest expression of historical and spiritual reality depends upon its acceptance as the inner life of the knowing spirit and not an external authority. The alienation of the human spirit from this tradition would denote the external imposition of the latter. But we ought to conceive tradition as man's inner, free and spiritual tie; as something that is neither transcendental nor imposed upon him but immanent. This is the only conception of tradition that contains the true basis of a philosophy.

Let us now approach the problem of what constitutes the essence of the historical from another standpoint. How did the idea of the 'historical' arise in the history of the human consciousness and human spirit? How did the human consciousness first grasp the historical process and fulfilment? How did it first become aware that history fulfilled itself, that there existed an everyday reality which we term the historical world, the historical movement and the historical process? To answer these questions we must go back to the Hellenic and Hebraic worlds.

Both the Hellenic and the Hebraic principles enter closely into the constitution of the European consciousness; their organic union in the Christian world had helped to inaugurate a new era. It is clear, I think, to any student of history that the Hellenic culture, world and consciousness were lacking in historical sense. They had no conception of history as fulfilling itself. Even the greatest Greek philosophers were unaware of the 'historical' and the possibility of a philosophy of history. Neither Plato nor Aristotle nor any of the other great philosophers has left us a conception of history. This is the result, I think, of the way in which the Greeks interpreted the world. They conceived the world aesthetically, as a finite and harmonious cosmos. The most representative Hellenic thinkers conceived creation as something static, as a sort of classical contemplation of a well-ordered cosmos. This is true of all the great Greek philosophers, who could grasp neither the historical process nor that of historical fulfilment. To them history had no issue, no goal, no begin-

[27]

ning even; in it everything was recurrent, eternally rotating and governed by a cyclic motion. The Hellenic consciousness was, in fact, never concerned with the future in which history fulfils itself and in which lie both its centre and issue, but only with the past. This view of futurity contained no basis for a conception of the historical process in general and of its fulfilment as a specific drama in particular.

For history is a drama which has its acts and logical development, its dénouement and catharsis. But this conception of history as tragedy was foreign to the Hellenic consciousness. Its origins must be sought rather in the consciousness and spirit of ancient Israel. It was the Jews who contributed the concept of 'historical' to world history, thereby discharging, in my opinion, the essence of their specific mission. They were the first to conceive the world as historical fulfilment in contradistinction to the cyclic process of the Greeks. For the ancient Hebrews the idea of fulfilment was always closely allied to that of Messianism. The Jewish consciousness, unlike that of the Greeks, always aspired towards the future; it lived in the intense expectation of some great decisive event in the destinies of Israel and of other peoples. It did not conceive the destiny of the world as a finite cyclic process. For the Jews the idea of history turns upon the expectation of some future event which will bring with it a solution of history. They are the first to demonstrate the structural character of the historical process and to become conscious of the 'historical'. And we must therefore seek the origins of the philosophy of history in Jewish rather than in Greek philosophy.

The Book of Daniel represents such a philosophy of history. In it we are made to feel dramatically that mankind is engaged in a process that tends towards a definite goal.

Daniel's interpretation of Nebuchadnezzar's dream represents the first attempt in the history of mankind to attribute a design to history—an attempt which was later to be repeated and developed in the Christian philosophy. The prophet Jeremiah's view of history is coloured by his belief that God chastised the peoples. He loved Nebuchadnezzar as the instrument of God. This prophetic character of the Jewish consciousness, its preoccupation with the future, helped not only to build up the philosophy of history but also to give birth to the very idea of the 'historical' itself. The Hellenic world had been content to contemplate a harmonious cosmos; but this was foreign to the Jews who were destined to reveal the historical drama of human destiny,—a drama depending on the fulfilment of some great event in the destiny of the Jewish people and of mankind as a whole. That was the Messianic idea peculiar to the Jewish people. It constitutes their specific contribution to the history of the human spirit.

I should like to make a few comparisons in illustration of this view. How was it that the Greeks, who contributed such great revelations to the human spirit, neither knew nor were capable of knowing the idea of history or of the 'historical'? Simply because, in my opinion, the Hellenic world possessed no real knowledge of freedom. Neither Greek religion nor Greek philosophy evinced any real sense of freedom. Submission to fate is the most characteristic feature of the Hellenic spirit. It had no conscious knowledge of freedom, that freedom of the subject to create history, without which neither its fulfilment nor comprehension is possible. We may attribute this to the preponderance which form had always exercised over content in the Hellenic world. In art, philosophy and politics, in every sphere of Hellenic life, the prin-

[29]

ciples of formal perfection always predominated over those of matter and content involving the irrational motive of human life. Now this irrational principle is synonymous with that of freedom as subsequently formulated by Christianity. The Christian world stressed content rather than form; it revealed that irrational principle underlying human freedom and the free creative subject without which the fulfilment of the historical process is impossible. The Christian consciousness, resting on the Jewish in so far as the latter discovered the 'historical', revealed that freedom of evil without which it is impossible either to grasp or approach the historical process. For there could be no history without that freedom of evil which derives from the primal origins of human life, as there could be none without these dark origins themselves. A world without these conditions would be world without beginning, mere fulfilment, the perfect Kingdom of God, a perfect cosmos in the form of perfect good and beauty. But the history of the world did not originate in this perfection, but rather in the freedom of evil. That is the idea behind the conception of the historical process, an idea which could not have proceeded from the Hellenic consciousness which was primarily concerned with the perfection of the cosmos.

The 'historical' and the metaphysical can never be identical to a purely abstract Aryan consciousness or monism. It is no accident that such contemporary thinkers and so-called representatives of the pure Aryan spirit as Chamberlain and Drevs, a philosopher of the Hartmann school, establish a profound antithesis between the metaphysical and the historical. Their whole criticism of the Semitic element in Christianity is based upon the fact that it constitutes, for them, an unlawful union between the metaphysical and the historical. This implies, of course, an admission that the metaphysical has become merged and materialised in historical facts, that it has become inalienably part of the historical. This purely Aryan consciousness tends to go back not to the Hellenic but to the Hindoo form of culture, which was the expression, perhaps, of a stricter and purer form of the Aryan spirit, and there seeks the inspiration of a purely metaphysical expression absolutely free from and unadulterated by historical premisses. The Hindoo consciousness and destiny are the most unhistorical in the world. Their most profound elements are untouched by history. They had no conception of history or of the historical process; their spiritual life appeared to be, above all, an individual one, an individual spiritual destiny, in the depths of which the higher world and the Divinity are revealed in a particular form that transcends historical destiny. The Hindoo spirit establishes an antithesis between the historical and the metaphysical; the abstraction of historical reality, of historical destiny, seemed to guarantee the purity of consciousness, since every restriction tended only to obscure the working of the spirit. The inability to bring about the union of the metaphysical and the historical led the Hindoos to conceive history as a mere external chain of phenomena devoid of any inner purpose or significance. History therefore becomes synonymous with the external empirical world, a base order of reality which it is necessary to master and renounce in order to achieve communion with the metaphysical essence of that higher world which bears the stamp of the spirit. Such then is the purely Aryan monism which we usually find opposed to the dualism of the Jewish and Christian consciousness.

[31]

The philosophy of history is in its origins intimately allied to eschatology; and this helps to explain its rise among the Jewish people. Eschatology is the doctrine of the goal of history, its issue and fulfilment. It is absolutely essential for the conception and elaboration of the idea of history, as a significant progression or movement capable of fulfilment. No conception of history is feasible without the idea of fulfilment because history is essentially eschatological; it postulates a final solution and issue, it presupposes a catastrophic fulfilment which inaugurates a new world and a new reality utterly different from the world and reality familiar to the Greeks, who had no eschatological sense. As an historical confirmation of this we may note that of all the peoples of the ancient world only the Jews and Persians evinced the least awareness of history and the historical destiny. The Persians were the only Aryan people to become aware of the 'historical', and this was due to the nature of their religious consciousness in which the eschatological element plays an important part. Their apocalypticism too influenced that of the Jews. Priority in the matter of the eschatological belongs to the Persians. They are the only people besides the Jews who saw the historical destiny as a determinate end and fulfilment. The conflict between Ormuz and Ariman is resolved by a catastrophe which brings about the end of history and the beginning of something else. Without this sense of an end, the process cannot be conceived as historical movement. Without this eschatological perspective progression cannot be considered as history, for it lacks inner purpose, significance and fulfilment. And ultimately, a progression that neither leads towards a determinate end nor has any such end in view tends to be governed by cyclic motion. To deprive the historical process of all significance is to make its very conception impossible.

The Jewish people were the first to have an inkling of a philosophy of history. But it was reserved for the Christian world to establish a real philosophy of history as a particular category of spiritual knowledge and *Weltanschauung*. Christianity blended in itself all the confessions of the world, the Hellenic as well as the Jewish, and it alone possessed that peculiar intuition of the 'historical' which was denied to the classical and even perhaps the Jewish worlds. In one of his most interesting and illuminating thoughts Schelling suggested that Christianity is in the highest degree historical and represented a revelation of God in history. The tie between Christianity and history is such as exists in no other world religion. Christianity introduced historical dynamism and the extraordinary force of historical movement, and thus made possible a philosophy of history. It laid the foundations not only of the Christian philosophy of history in the religious sense of philosophies like those of St. Augustine or Bossuet, but also of all subsequent philosophies of history down to that of Marx himself. And indeed the dynamism peculiar to the latter belongs essentially to a Christian period of history.

The dynamism introduced by Christianity derived from its idea of the immediacy and uniqueness of events which was foreign to the pagan world. The latter had, on the contrary, been dominated by the idea of the frequency and recurrence of events, and this had made all conception of history impossible. The Christian consciousness, on the other hand, held that events were immediate, non-recurrent and unique, and it imposed this conception on historical reality. For it was convinced that an event of central importance in history

[33]

had taken place; an event that had been completed once and for all; a non-recurring, indivisible, incomparable and unique event that was both historical and metaphysical, and that revealed the depths of life; in a word, Christ's revelation.

History is a progression; it possesses an inner significance and mystery, a point of departure and a goal, a centre and a purpose. It both ends and begins with the fact of Christ's Revelation. This fact determines both the profound dynamism of history and its movement towards and away from the heart of universal history. The Hellenic world ignored the possibility of such a conception, of such an historical as well as metaphysical fact, because its divinities were remote from the temporal process of history. Truth, the divine values and the divine harmony were revealed to the Hellenic consciousness only in eternal nature. The Greeks had no knowledge of the historical progression which carries the universe towards a catastrophic event.

History and its conception are possible only when the world process is conceived as a catastrophic one. The catastrophic interpretation of history postulates a central fact,— that of the divine revelation, by which the interior becomes the exterior and the Spirit incarnate. Such a conception was foreign to the Hellenic consciousness and even more so to the profoundly spiritual consciousness of India, which had no presentiment whatsoever of a great central event in history. In India all the values of spiritual life were revealed only in the individual depths of the human spirit. Christianity first introduced that conception of freedom which had been ignored by the Hellenic world but which was essential to the building up of the idea of history and of its philosophy. It is impossible to conceive history without such an understanding of freedom, which centres on history its dramatic and tragic character, the tragedy of free action, evil and darkness. This fact determines the dramatic conflict and movement of history, unsuspected by the Hellenic mind with its view of good, beauty and truth as divinely essential. But because it first acknowledged that the eternal can have a temporal fulfilment, Christianity brought us the contribution of both history and its idea. The eternal and the temporal both coexist in the Christian consciousness in reciprocal participation. While the Greek consciousness had conceived the time process as a cycle, Christianity passed beyond the cyclic idea, asserted the progression of history in time and discovered an historical purpose. It introduced the notion of dynamism and the liberating principle which released that tempestuous and rebellious history of the Western peoples which has become pre-eminently history.

Compared with the destiny of the non-Christian peoples, whether ancient or contemporary, that of the Christian peoples is associated with all the important events in history and with its very core. This is the result of the freedom and dynamism which Christianity introduced through its insistence upon the unique character of historical and metaphysical facts. It heightened the intensity of the historical process and introduced a particular violence of inner drama and rhythm which had been lacking in the history of all non-Christian peoples with the possible exception of the Jews. Consequently a great and distinct Christian world evolved— a world that was dynamic by contrast with the static world of antiquity. The latter had been founded upon an immanence of being and of life; its consciousness apprehended the existence only of a finite cupola of the heavens beneath and within which flowed the whole of human life; it ignored trans-cendental flights and expanses; and all beauty, all the beauty of spiritual and divine life, was revealed to it only as an immanence through the movement of the cycles. The Christian world, on the other hand, discovered expanses and passed beyond the cupola of heaven; and its urge towards the outer spaces gave rise to that dynamism and drama of history which drew into their vortex even those peoples and nations which, though now estranged from the Christian consciousness, have yet remained Christian and historical in their destiny.

There are grounds for supposing that the revolt against Christianity in the nineteenth and twentieth centuries was based upon the active principles implicit in Christianity. Thus its associations can be traced back to the dynamism, the freedom and the irrational principles of vital activity, which break through all limitations and determine the historical process. This dynamic and historical character is peculiar to Christianity, which alone attributed a general and ultimate goal to mankind. It achieved the unity of the latter and thus laid the foundations of the philosophy of history. As I have already pointed out, historical reality implies the existence of an irrational principle which makes dynamism possible. Neither history nor true dynamism is possible without this principle, which is turbulent, mobile and pliant, and which kindles the conflict between the opposing forces of light and darkness. We should think of this irrational principle not in the gnosiological sense attributed to it by Rikkert, who establishes an opposition between the particular as an irrational force and the general as a rational one, but rather ontological-ly as the *sine qua non* of freedom and dynamism.

History postulates a Divine-humanity. The character of

the religious and historical process presupposes a profound clash and interaction between the Divinity and man, between Providence, divine fatality and necessity on the one hand, and the unfathomable mystery of human freedom on the other. There would be no drama of history, no tragic development, expressing the profound clash, interaction and strife between the Divinity and mankind on the ground of freedom, if only one principle, that of natural or divine necessity, were involved. But these two principles are irreconcilable; they form an antinomy, an antithesis. And their opposition in the human spirit can be explained only in terms of the Christian consciousness. There would be no universal history without the freedom of the human spirit conceived as an autonomous principle independent of either divine freedom or divine necessity; and one that is both irrational and unfathomable. History in the true sense of the word could neither exist nor be conceived on the isolated basis of divine freedom or divine necessity on the one hand, or, again, natural necessity on the other. The exclusive existence of the divine necessity, the divine principle or the divine freedom would make history begin with the Kingdom of God, and there would therefore be no history. Similarly, the exclusive action of natural necessity would result in a meaningless chain of exterior facts devoid of all inner fulfilment, and all tragic and dramatic design. Therefore every monistic philosophy, every pure monism, which admits the existence of only one principle, is unfavourable both to the building up of a philosophy of history and to the apprehension of its dynamism. Pure monism is essentially anti-historical and has always tended to deny both human freedom and the irrational freedom of evil as the religious and metaphysical *a priori* of history.

I should like to consider several other aspects of the question in support of my fundamental premiss and conception of the philosophy of history. In the first place, I should like to dwell upon a false approach very prevalent in the contemporary consciousness, which tends to transform history into an inert mass of material devoid of inner life and meaning. One of the great fallacies of the contemporary consciousness lies in the anti-historical and anarchical revolt of the individual personality which, as a result of its divorce and isolation from the 'historical', attacks the historical process as a tyranny. This position, however, does not ultimately emancipate man, but only enslaves him. For he who rebels against the great divine and human content of history, asserts it to be something not organic and inwardly revealed, but imposed upon him from without. Such a rebellious and anarchical attitude is founded upon a slavish state of the spirit. For freedom of the spirit belongs only to him who no longer feels history as an exterior imposition, and who begins to apprehend it as an interior event of spiritual significance, that is, as the expression of freedom. Only in such a free and emancipating view can history be understood as the expression of man's inner freedom and a phase in his celestial and terrestrial destiny. In it man follows his peculiar path of martyrdom upon which all the great moments of history, the most terrible as well as the most torturing, appear as the interior moments of the human destiny; for history represents the interior and dramatic fulfilment of the latter. And only those who refuse to see the historical process as the fulfilment of a great human destiny and are content to regard it as a merely superficial and exterior process will behold the void of history and not its truth.

[38]

History unites two elements, the creative and the conservative. The historical process would not be possible without their union. By the conservative element I mean a tie with the spiritual past, an inner tradition, and an acceptance of the sacred heritage of the past. But history also demands a dynamic-creative element, a creative sequence and purpose, an urge towards self-fulfilment. Thus the free audacity of the creative principle coexists with an inner tie and a profound communion with the past. The absence of either of these elements invalidates the postulate of history.

Pure and abstract conservatism is anti-historical since it claims that its function is to preserve what has already been accomplished. Such a view makes the apprehension of history impossible. On the other hand, a tie with the past and what is sacred in it is one with the creative dynamism of life; fidelity to the covenants of the past is fidelity to those of our ancestors' creative and dynamic life. A tie therefore with our ancestors, with our native land, with all that is sacred, is one with the creative and dynamic process which is addressing itself to the future, determining the fulfilment and creation of a new world and life, and effecting the union between the new world of the future and the old world of the past. The process occurs in eternity; and the union in eternal life fulfils itself in a sort of unique, historical, creative and dynamic movement. Such a conception favours the union of the temporal and the eternal, of the historical and the metaphysical, of that which is present in the physical facts of history and that which has been revealed in the inmost depths of spiritual reality; and it helps to knit together terrestrial and celestial history.

What do we understand by celestial history? In it, in the

depths of the inner life of the spirit, resides that predetermination which reveals and manifests itself in the terrestrial life, destiny and history of mankind. This heavenly prologue is analogous to that which opens Goethe's *Faust*. Faust's destiny is that of man; and this heavenly prologue predetermines the terrestrial destiny of mankind. The philosophy of history ought to be the metaphysics of history; it has its origins in that heavenly prologue which predetermines historical destinies and in the revelation of the inner spiritual history; for heaven is our inner spiritual heaven. Here is to be found that true tie between the historical and the metaphysical in which I see the deepest significance of every Christian philosophy of history. It transcends cleavage and antithesis; it achieves the maximum union, reconciliation and identification; and it brings about the mysterious adaptation and transfiguration of the one into the other, of the heavenly into the terrestrial, of the metaphysical into the historical, of the interior into the exterior.

The philosophy of history attempts to define the historical process; it is a sort of reversed prophecy. It reveals no objective hypothesis; nor does it consist in the apprehension of historical facts. It is the prophetic exegesis of both the past and the future; for the metaphysic of past history is revealed like that of the future, and inversely. A cleavage between them precipitates us into darkness and makes the historical process unintelligible. Such a cleavage is effected by all those who feel themselves to be divorced from the great historical past and who have no knowledge of the great historical future, who feel that the former has been imposed upon them, and who fear the latter and all it contains as something unfathomable, inaccessible and unintelligible.

To this view we oppose that which seeks to establish a tie between historical and human destiny, to bind past and future in eternity. In this way the inner forces of history, which are concealed from those who extend a static conception of the present into both past and future, reveal themselves. To interpret past and future neither from the standpoint of their dynamic relation nor from that of their inner and spiritual connection and fulfilment, but as separate, abstract and lifeless entities, is to be guilty of a falsification. Such a standpoint, however revolutionary it may appear, is an essentially static one. For the static present, in which the knowing subject finds itself once he has broken away from both past and future, from their interior sequence of movement and fulfilment, impedes the apprehension of reality and transforms the past into a lifeless and mechanical process. History stands still and settles in the past. Only a prophetic vision of the past can set history in motion; and only a prophetic vision of the future can bind the present and the past into a sort of interior and complete spiritual movement. Only a prophetic vision can re-animate the dead body of history and inform the lifeless static with the inner fire of spiritual movement.

The human destiny is both terrestrial and celestial. It is not only an historical but also a metaphysical, not only a human but also a divine destiny; it is not only a human but also a divine drama. Only a prophetic attitude to history can make lifeless evolution and movement both active and inwardly inspired. It seems to me that the significance of this ought now to be clear to all. The fundamental conclusion I reach in the course of my investigation of the nature of history and its philosophy is that no opposition between man and history, between man's spiritual world and the great world of history, can exist. The result of such an opposition would only be to deprive both man and history of all life.

The metaphysics of history, which ought to be our goal, does not consider history as an object, as an exterior object of cognition, as a mere manifestation of the exterior world of objects. It implies, on the contrary, insight into the depths and very essence of history; it implies the discovery of history in the reality of its inner life, drama, movement and fulfilment; in brief, it has to do with a subject-object. My present lectures are permeated with this sense of the union of the historical subject and object.

Such a conception of history is designed to destroy one of the current delusions and aberrations whereby a cleavage and opposition are set up between history on earth and that 'hereafter'. This aberration is due to the fact that we tend to argue from our own time to the dawn and primordial history of mankind. We draw a sharp line of demarcation between the historical and the metaphysical, between terrestrial and celestial history. But this distinction does not reflect the true reality and forms but an abstraction of our consciousness. Indeed, all that occurred at the dawn of human history, all that is reflected in the Bible and in mythology (mythology, according to Schelling, constitutes the primordial history of mankind), is not merely a stage in an historical time-process that resembles our terrestrial one; for in the remote past no frontiers between the terrestrial and the celestial existed. Biblical mythology treats of both man's terrestrial and celestial destiny, and of the mythological history of mankind; for, in the early history of mankind, no frontiers had been drawn between the two destinies. It is only later that they are distinguished, and it is then that the cleavage between the terrestrial and the celestial becomes apparent. It is upon the basis of this cleavage that we tend to reconstruct early history. But its inner and sacred nature can be apprehended only if we assume that neither this cleavage nor these frontiers existed, and that the first stage of man's terrestrial destiny had its origin in heaven; that it was born in a sort of spiritual reality which was at the same time an historical one, rich in monuments and other data for the researches of historical science, criticism, and archaeology. The metaphysics of history, on the other hand, approaches man's destiny from the standpoint of the inner intimacy and union subsisting between his celestial and terrestrial destinies.

CHAPTER III

OF CELESTIAL HISTORY: GOD AND MAN

Man's celestial history and destiny predetermine his terrestrial. The theme of universal history is given us in the heavenly prologue. But what do we mean by celestial history? It is the true metaphysical foundation of history. Heaven and the heavenly life in which the historical process originates constitute the deepest interior spiritual life. For heaven is not a remote transcendental and unattainable sphere; it is a part of the inmost depths of our spiritual life. When we dive below the surface and penetrate into these depths we then really commune with celestial life. In them is stored a spiritual experience which differs from that of terrestrial reality and which represents a deeper and more spacious stratum of being. In it, in this interior spiritual reality, in this experience of the human spirit, which is neither remote nor antithetical but in direct communion with the divine spirit, lies the source of history. And in it too is revealed the drama of the mutual relations between God and man. The celestial is that deepest reality which propounds the theme of man's relations with God and the absolute source of life.

This relationship constitutes that deeper sphere which contains the origins of history, its seed and the predetermination of its fundamental aspects. For it follows that if history is more than a mere external phenomenon, if it possesses

[44]

some absolute significance or tie with absolute life, if it is based upon a true ontological principle, then it must have both its beginning and fulfilment in the inmost depths of the Absolute, that is, in those depths of being with which spiritual life and ultimate spiritual experience at their deepest come into communion. To admit, therefore, that the historical process is predetermined in the depths of spiritual life, is to admit its origin in the depths of the Absolute, in the divine life itself. The latter in a deep and mysterious sense is history, historical drama and mystery. Only a logical and absolutely abstract monism can deny this character of drama and mystery, which motivates and fulfils historical destiny within divine life. Only it can conceive the Divine Being as something absolutely immobile and opposed to every process, dramatic action, interior tragedy of passions and clash of deepest spiritual forces. An abstract monism of this sort admits of movement only in the imperfect plural world. And this world is phenomenal, empirical, unreal, secondary and merely manifest,— one of multiple movement and tragic conflicts which give birth to historical destiny. Monism regards this world as one merely of appearance and illusion, having no real existence. It associates movement only with the relative world and leaves the Absolute and the divine life unaffected by it.

In this way a consistent monism brings about a cleavage between the depths of spiritual life and the nature of the Divine Being, on the one hand, and the plural, contradictory and mobile world in the process of fulfilling history, on the other. But it is based upon an unresolvable inner contradiction. The nature of the historical destiny of this interior world proves such that not only can it not be transposed into the inmost depths of divine life, but it can in no way communicate with it. No form of abstract monism is therefore capable of explaining inwardly the origin of the plural world. For how is it possible to explain the origin and formation of that plural corrupt world, in which the historical process occurs, in whose vortex we are whirled and whose destiny we share, in the inmost depths of the absolute life of an immobile and unique Deity? How are we to explain its origin in this so-called absolute life to which no form of human movement, principle or plurality, conflicts or clashes, are applicable? Neither the pantheistic monism of the Hindoo type, which regards the world as an illusion; nor Parmenides; nor Plato, who was unable to bridge the dualism of the unique-immobile and the plural-mobile; nor Plotinus; nor, finally, the abstract monism of German idealism, were able to achieve it. It remains an insoluble mystery to them all.

Ultimately, these systems must arrive at some form of acosmism, that is, they must acknowledge the real existence of a unique, absolute and immobile Divinity and consider the mobile plural world with its interior contradictions as unreal in the ontological sense of the word. It is interesting to observe, however, that the disciples of abstract monism tend, ironically enough, to fall into an unresolvable dualism of their own. They introduce such a sharp distinction between the unique, immobile and absolutely perfect Divinity, on the one hand, and the world of man, movement, historical destiny, tragic conflicts, plurality and contradiction, on the other; they introduce such an antithesis and make it so impossible to bridge the gap between its poles, that they establish another extreme and unresolvable form of dualism. The only way to escape it is to deny that form of monism which recognizes only the unique and immobile Absolute as truly existing. Thus every philosophy and form of religious consciousness, which admits both the monistic and the dualist state, surmounts the hopelessness of such a dualism. It bridges the gap between the two worlds, grasps the significance of plurality and considers the tragic experience of man and the world in relation to the destiny of the Absolute itself and the interior drama implicit, predetermined and fulfilled in its depths.

How is such a conception of the nature of the divine life in the two fundamental aspects I have attempted to distinguish related to the Christian consciousness? That is both a complex and debatable question. For, according to the dogma of the Church and its prevailing philosophy, the possibility of movement or of an historical process in the depths of divine life would appear to be incompatible with the Christian consciousness. There exists, indeed, a widespread Christian doctrine which denies that the principle of movement and of tragic destiny can affect the nature of the Divine Being. But I am deeply convinced that the Christian doctrine of the immobility and inertia of God and the Absolute, and of the effectiveness of the historical principle only in the created and relative world that differs essentially from the Absolute, is a purely exoteric and superficial doctrine. And it ignores what is most inward and mysterious, the esoteric truth implicit in the doctrine of the Divinity.

It may even be said that such a doctrine, which fears to admit the mobility of the divine life subject to its own inner tragedy, is in blatant contradiction with the fundamental Christian mysteries of the Divine Trinity, of Christ as the centre of divine life and of Golgotha. For Christianity in its inmost depths understands the essence of being and true

[47]

reality as an interior mystery, drama and tragedy, which is at the same time a divine tragedy. The destiny of the Crucified Son of God constitutes the deepest mystery of Christianity. For the tragic passionate mystery experienced by the Divine Being presupposes the transposition of the principle of mobility and of interior tragic conflict into the nature of the inner divine life. If Christ, the Son of God, suffers a tragic destiny, and if historical destiny and movement are also manifest in Him, then this constitutes a recognition of the tragedy experienced by the divine life. For it is impossible to assert the tragic destiny of the Son of God and His expiatory death without at the same time admitting movement in the divine life. In the same way the Christian consciousness makes it possible to transpose the principle of tragic movement to the interior nature of the Divinity. The type of pure monism, which denies the Divine Trinity or considers that its recognition introduces plurality into the divine life, particularly favours the view that no movement can exist in the interior nature of the Divine Being. And yet the whole mystery of Christianity is contained in the principle of the Trinity and in the fulfilment of a passionate tragic destiny within it. This conception of the nature of the Absolute predetermines for Christianity the creation of the world itself. God the Son is the justification of the latter. And the creation of the world by God the Father is a moment of the deepest mystery in the relation between God the Father and God the Son. The revelation of the divine mystery in the depths of the divine and spiritual life, of the inner passionate divine thirst and longing for an other self, that other self which may be the object of a great and infinite love on the part of God, and that infinite thirst for reciprocity and love on the part of the other self, determines for the deep Christian consciousness the very principle of movement and process. This inner tragedy of the love felt by God for His other self and its longing for reciprocal love constitutes that very mystery of the divine life which is associated with the creation of the world and of man.

This creation represented such an interior movement and dramatic history in the divine life; it was the history of the divine love between God and His other self. And thus the Second Person of the Divine Trinity, the Son of God and symbol of infinite love, is the very heart of both the divine and the world tragedy and destiny. Herein is accomplished the union of the historical destinies of the divine and human lives. Without such a conception of divine and spiritual life it is impossible to grasp the origins of history or the true destiny of the world and of mankind. And it is based essentially upon a dynamic interpretation of the depths of spiritual life as a creative movement and tragic destiny.

Has the conception of spiritual life and reality as something immobile, inert and antithetical to all historical destiny, any foundation? That, in my opinion, constitutes one of the fundamental problems of religion and philosophy. It is a problem which has deeply marked the whole history of human self-consciousness, opposing the dynamic and static conceptions of spiritual reality. Greek philosophy had already established the fundamental types of philosophical approach which were to be developed in later history; and it offers us the models of both these types. Thus Parmenides and the Eleatic philosophers conceived the deepest spiritual and divine reality, that is, the true metaphysical reality, as something that was unique and immobile. But Heraclitus, one of the greatest of philosophers, conceived it as fiery movement.

The whole history of philosophy bears witness to the clash and conflict of these two types. And, it must be added, the Parmenides type, which advocates the doctrine of immobility and of the stasis of true being, and of the metaphysically unreal and non-existent world of movement, has generally predominated. As a matter of fact, it has helped to prevent the Christian consciousness from comprehending the dynamism of the divine life which it regarded as immobile and antithetical to historical destinies. This philosophical tradition is, however, irreconcilably opposed to the Christian mystery of the passion and sufferings of the Divine Son and of His historical destiny.

The usual philosophical objection to the possibility of movement in the interior depths of the Absolute is a formalist and rationalistic one. It reduces itself to the argument that such an assumption is irreconcilable with divine perfection, since all movement, destiny and history postulate an insufficiency and, hence, an imperfection. The supposition that there exists within the divine life a sort of need and longing which have not yet been satisfied, and which therefore point to the imperfection of the Absolute itself, is inadmissible. But this rationalistic objection can hardly impose itself or appear to be particularly adequate as an interpretation of the mystery of the divine life. In fact, it denies the interior antinomy of all theosophy. It is a superficial rationalistic interpretation of nature which gives birth to a still-born deism or abstract monism which can in general apprehend neither the origins nor the destiny of the world process. The very opposite might, indeed, be affirmed with as great success. It might be argued that the absence of creative movement, of creative historical destiny in the inmost depths of the Absolute, also denotes an insufficiency and imperfection in it. For creative movement, indeed, represents not only the fulfilment of insufficiency and the existence of as yet unfulfilled demands, but is also the proof of the perfection of being.

All being devoid of creative movement would suffer a loss; it would be denied creative destiny and history. Therefore the above objection, which is widely current in official dogmatic Christian philosophy, is vitiated by limited rationalistic thought and contradicts the nature of the Divine Being. For the knowledge of Absolute life can only be attained through the recognition of the antinomy of this life. This contradiction is the sign that we are communing with the deepest mystery of spiritual life, which we cannot approach through the superficial criteria of formal logic. The real way to approach spiritual reality and the knowledge of the divine life, which holds all the threads of universal and human history, is not through abstract philosophy but through concrete mythology.

It is a matter of the greatest importance to distinguish between these approaches to the mysteries of the spiritual and the divine life. As we have seen, the latter cannot be solved by any abstract philosophy. A more perfect type of philosophy is that which enters into the framework of abstract monism; for the types of Spinozian, Hindoo and even Hegelian (with certain developments, it is true, since it envisages a process in the Absolute) monism are the least contradictory and the most perfected philosophies of the Divine. But this monism is deeply opposed to the essentials of the Christian consciousness. Nor can it in general resolve the problems of the world, those of a plural world, of its origins, history, tragic conflicts, destiny and inwardly experienced contradictions. I am therefore inclined to believe that the mysteries of the divine as well as of the human and world life, with all their complexity of historical destiny, admit of solution only through concrete mythology. The knowledge of the divine life is not attainable by means of abstract philosophical thought based upon the principles of formalist or rationalistic logic, but only by means of a concrete myth which conceives the divine life as a passionate destiny of concrete and active persons, the divine Hypostases.

This is, therefore, not a philosophy, but a mythology. The Gnostics had such a mythology. And that explains their success in apprehending, in spite of certain deficiencies and confusions in their thought, the divine mysteries as those of an historical destiny better than the abstract philosophers, who were content to remain within the framework of their philosophies. Such a mythology makes possible the apprehension of the essence of celestial history, of the stages, the aeons or ages of the divine life. The very conception of the divine aeons is bound up with concrete destiny and is essentially illusive and inapprehensible to any abstract philosophical system. Only a mythology, which conceives the divine celestial life as celestial history and as a drama of love and freedom unfolding itself between God and His other self, which He loves and for whose reciprocal love He thirsts, and only an admission of God's longing for His other self, can provide a solution of celestial history and, through it, of the destinies of both man and the world. Only such a freedom of both God and man, only such a divine and human love in the fulness of the tragic relationship, would appear to be the way to discover the sources of every historical destiny. Only in this way will the plot stand revealed.

We must not be afraid to emphasize the importance of anthropomorphism in this connection. For only such an inner apprehension of the divine life and destiny in their deepest relation to human destiny offers a solution of the divine mystery required by the metaphysics of history. Only this sort of concrete mythology can help us to apprehend those elements that the formalist approach of pantheistic monism cannot grasp. The latter is quite incapable of explaining man's origins or destiny, because it fails to situate the origin of the tragic movement associated with man's destiny in the inmost depths of a divine life which is not unique and immobile. But it is only by discovering the interior connection between the divine life and the tragedy of mankind that it becomes possible to grasp the significance of man's origin and destiny, that is, of the interior mutual relation between God and man. And this, indeed, solves the relations existing between God and the world. For man stands in the centre of the world and his destiny determines that of the world. Only this mystery of the mutual relations between God and man, of love and freedom, and of freely-given love, can elucidate the depths of the inner divine life and the mobile plural world.

To understand the interior relationship between God and man as a drama of freely-given love is to lay bare the sources of history. In fact, the whole of historical destiny can be reduced to that of man, which is in its turn the destiny of the deepest relationship subsisting between man and God, revealed simultaneously in both interior spiritual experience and exterior historical destinies. The one serves to illuminate the other, but only on condition that the divine life is interpreted as a drama between God and His other self, in the centre of which stands the Son of God, Who is both perfect God and man. The mystery of Christ is therefore that of the relations between God and man; it is the tragedy of freely-given love. But this is the sphere of mythology, in which I find not the negation, but the affirmation of reality. And thus mythology may offer a real key to the metaphysics of history.

I have so far been treating of questions that may appear to have little concern with the philosophy of history. But the connection will gradually become clear and the necessity of these hypotheses will be admitted. It will become obvious, too, why such primary problems of metaphysics are inseparable from a philosophy of history. And to illustrate still further my view that the origins of history lie in the inmost depths of the Absolute and in the tragic potential of divine life itself (and this constitutes the true hypothesis of the esoteric Christian philosophy of history), I shall deal briefly with the profound and original doctrine of German mysticism. This has, of course, exercised a great influence on German philosophy as a whole and especially on the concept of movement in the Absolute.

I am thinking of Boehme, who is not only a great German mystic, but also one of the greatest mystics of all time; and particularly of his *The Dark Nature of God*. Boehme's doctrine is closely connected with what I have been saying, and offers a concrete illustration of the fundamental hypothesis of the metaphysics of history. In fact, I believe it to be one of the most important discoveries of the German spirit, where it has not ceased to be applied and developed in the spheres of philosophy, art and culture in general. This spiritual culture is founded upon an apprehension of primal Being as a dark and irrational force of obscure origin (not in the sense of evil, for this darkness goes deeper than the distinctions between good and evil). Somewhere, in immeasurably greater depths, there exists a state which may be called *Ungrund* or 'groundlessness' to which neither human words nor the categories of good and evil nor those of being or non-being are applicable. *Ungrund* is deeper than anything else and is the primal source of what, according to Boehme and Schelling, constitutes the *Dark Nature of God*. In the nature of God, deeper than Him, lies a sort of primal dark abyss, and in its inmost depths occurs a theogonic process or that of divine genesis. This process is secondary when compared with that primal 'groundlessness' and inexpressible abyss which is irrational and incommensurable with any of our categories. There is a primal source and fount of being from which an eternal torrent pours and in which the divine light shines everlastingly, while the act of divine genesis is taking place.

The acceptance of such a dark and irrational premiss is one of the means towards the discovery and apprehension of the mystery of the possible existence of movement in the inmost depths of the divine life. For the fact of such a dark primal source and nature implies the possibility of tragic destiny for the divine life. And if the tragedy of passions has its place in the divine life and destiny in the centre of which stands the passion of God Himself and His Son; and if this, again, is an aid to Redemption; then it can only be explained by the existence of a profound source of such a tragic conflict, movement and passion in the depths of the divine life itself. Every glib rationalistic theory of the Divine denies this. All superficial doctrines, fearing to extend tragic movement to the divine life because they envisage the latter without inner contradiction or conflict, that is, reduced to an extreme form of logical and rational conception, also deny this. But it constitutes the great discovery of the German mystics in whose works it is stated most forcibly, if perhaps not for the first time in history. It determined to a large extent the future of German philosophy, whose fundamental discovery it indeed represents. It states that the primal foundations of being rest upon a certain irrational and wilful principle, and that the whole significance and essence of the world process consist in the illumination of this dark irrational principle in cosmogony and theogony. And this is the hypothesis of my metaphysics of history, that the terrestrial destiny is predetermined by the celestial, in which the tragedy of illumination and Redemption takes place through the divine passion, and that tragedy determines the process of illuminating world history.

This conception of the Absolute peculiar to German mysticism and philosophy, and particularly to Schelling and Baader, coincides with the deeper current of Christian thought. Before developing our metaphysics of history any further, we must pause to consider the primal drama and mystery taking place in the inmost depths of being. What is the nature of this drama? It is that of the mutual relations between God and man. But in what form are we to conceive it? I believe that this primal drama and mystery of Christianity consist in the genesis of God in man and of man in God. This mystery is, indeed, implicit in the foundations of Christianity. One or other aspect of it is revealed in the various periods of Christianity. Historical destiny reveals more particularly the genesis of God in man. This constitutes the central fact of human and world destiny. But there exists a no less profound mystery, that of the genesis of man in God, accomplished in the inmost depths of the divine life. For if there is such a thing as a human longing for God and a response to it, then there also must be a divine longing for man and the genesis of God in man; a longing for the loved and the freely-loving and, in response to it, the genesis of man in God. And thus the mystery of the anthropogonistic process is accomplished. A divine movement which brings about the genesis of God implies the reciprocal movement of man towards God, by which he is generated and revealed. This constitutes the primal mystery both of the spirit and of being, and at the same time of Christianity, which in its central fact, in the Person of Christ, the Son of God, unites two mysteries. In the Image of Christ is brought about the genesis of God in man and of man in God, and the perfection of both is manifest. Thus, for the first time, in response to God's movement and longing, a perfect man is revealed to Him. This mysterious process occurs in the interior depths of the divine reality itself; it is a sort of divine history which is reflected in the whole of the outer history of mankind. History is, indeed, not only the revelation of God, but also the reciprocal revelation of man in God.

The whole complexity of the historical process can be explained by the inner interdependence of these two revelations. For history is not only the plan of the Divine revelation, it is also the reciprocal revelation of man himself; and that makes history such a terrible and complex tragedy. History would not be tragic if it were only the revelation of God and its gradual apprehension. Its drama and tragedy are not only determined in the divine life itself, but also by the fact that they are based upon the mystery of freedom, which is not only a divine, but also a human revelation— that longed for by God in the depths of the divine life. The origin of the world springs from the freedom willed by God in the beginning. Without His will or longing for freedom no world process would be possible. In its place there would be a static and pre-eminently perfect Kingdom of God as an essential and predetermined harmony. The world process, on the other hand, implies a terrible tragedy, and history a succession of calamitous events in the centre of which stands the Crucifixion, the Cross on which the Son of God Himself was crucified, because God had desired freedom and because the primal drama and mystery of the world are those of the relations between God and His other self, which He loves and by which He desires to be loved. And only freedom endows this love with any significance.

This freedom, which is absolutely irrational and inapprehensible to reason, offers a solution of the tragedy of world history. It fulfils not only God's revelation in man, but also man's in God; for it is the source and origin of movement, of process, of inner conflict and of inwardly experienced contradictions. An indissoluble tie exists therefore between freedom and the metaphysics of history. The concept of freedom elucidates both the divine life as a tragic destiny and the life of mankind and the world as the history of a tragic destiny. There would be no history without freedom. It is the metaphysical basis of history. The revelation of history can be apprehended only through Christ as perfect man and God, as their perfect union, as the genesis of God in man and of man in God, and, finally, as God's revelation in man and the reciprocal revelation of man in God. Christ, the Absolute

[58]

Man, the Son of both God and man, stands in the centre of both celestial and terrestrial history. He is the inner spiritual tie between these two destinies. Without His help the tie between the world and God, between the plural and the unique, between the human and the absolute reality, could not exist. In fact, history owes its existence entirely to the presence of Christ at its very heart. He represents the deepest mystical and metaphysical foundation and source of history and of its tragic destiny. Both the divine and the human energy flow towards and away from Him. Without Him this energy would neither exist nor possess any significance.

History originates among the Jewish people because the latter had a mystical presentiment of the tie between celestial and terrestrial history. The coming of Christ put an end to the cleavage between the metaphysical and the historical which become united and identified in Him. Thus the metaphysical becomes the historical and vice versa; and celestial becomes terrestrial history which can be apprehended as a stage of the former. The conception, too, of the primal drama and mystery of being as that of freely-given love and freedom desired by God is, in terms of mythology rather than abstract philosophy, the inversion of God's desire and longing for man. God's desire for man implies that He desires his freely-given love. And this constitutes both the foundation and theme of world history and destiny. I shall expand upon this fact when discussing the primal mystery and its tragic fulfilment in the various stages of world history. For freely-given love, indeed, offers not only the theme but also the solution of world history along the path of freedom rather than of necessity. It endows history, however, with that terrible and disastrous character which compels many to doubt the existence of Providence and to conclude that the whole of world history is but a refutation of It. Such a terrible destiny, such a triumph of a secular premiss of evil over good, would seem irreconcilable with the existence of a Providence. This objection, however, becomes not only invalid but an actual proof of our thesis if we conceive the Divine Being Himself and the primal mystery of life as the mystery of freely-given love. It is precisely the tragic and tortured destiny of world history which evinces the inner mystery of love implicit within the unfathomable mystery of freedom, as the source of all those tortures in the life of the world and man to which necessity or divine constraint could easily put an end.

But this would contradict the Divine Will regarding the fulfilment of human destiny in freely-given love. Therefore all historical tendencies which have striven to create harmony, to overcome the dark premiss, to subdue the turbulence of freedom and supersede it by compelled and necessary good, are concerned only with the secondary signs of the unique and primal mystery of divine freedom. These tendencies have a wide currency, but they should be unmasked in the light of Christian consciousness as a temptation always besetting human destiny. One of the greatest of Christian mysteries, that of Grace, which lies at the foundation of the Church, symbolizes the transcendent reconciliation and resolution of the fatal conflict between freedom and necessity. It achieves a victory over the fatality of both freedom and necessity, though the word 'fatal' here is but an imperfect symbol. It is the act of Grace which realizes the communion between God and man and offers a solution of the problem posed by the divine drama. We must, therefore, note that the principle of Divine Grace is active in the history and destiny of both world and man together with that of natural necessity. And without it neither this destiny nor mystery would be fulfilled.

It constitutes the basis of every Christian philosophy of history, whose main object is the revelation of man in history. Thus history is made up of the complex interaction of the three principles of necessity, freedom and transfiguring Grace. Their inter-relation determines the whole complexity of man's historical destiny, and they can claim to be the motivating metaphysical forces in history. The whole course of humanism, on which I shall dwell later, clearly demonstrates the interaction of these principles. Indeed, the whole of the world process is governed by its relation to man whose destiny is its core, though it is, in its turn, predetermined by the divine drama. The solution of the fundamental problem of the metaphysics of history can come only from a myth which situates world destiny as a stage of the divine destiny in man, and thus predetermines its main spiritual forces.

The explanation of history as an interior metaphysical and spiritual, and not an anti-metaphysical, principle can be based only on a tie between the theogonic, cosmogonic and anthropogonic processes. This tie unites and integrates our spiritual experience. And this latter, if really profound, discloses the link between the metaphysical and the historical, the deeper spiritual, celestial, reality, on the one hand, and terrestrial reality, on the other. The solution it offers of human destiny as governed by the divine is at the same time a solution of both terrestrial and celestial history. This brings us to complex problems of a different order; to the nature of time

[61]

and its relation to eternity, and to the relation between the past and the future. These problems constitute the further hypotheses without which a real metaphysics of history is impossible.

CHAPTER IV

OF CELESTIAL HISTORY: TIME AND
ETERNITY

The nature and significance of time are the fundamental problem and premiss of every philosophy of history. For history is a process, movement and fulfilment within time. The significance we attach to history is directly determined by that which we attribute to time. But does time possess any metaphysical significance? Does it form part of that reality which penetrates into the inmost depths of being? Or is it but the condition and form of the manifest or phenomenal world? Does it form a part of real being or is it merely phenomenological, that is, bound up only with appearances without permeating the interior reality and the core of being? Every metaphysical system, however, which regards the 'historical' as something essential to the inmost depths of being, is bound to recognize the ontological significance of time, that is, the doctrine that time exists for the very essence of being. And this brings us to the problem of the relation of time and eternity.

To all appearances an insurmountable antithesis exists between time and eternity, and no relation can well be established between them. From this standpoint, time constitutes a sort of denial of eternity; it is a state which can have no roots in eternal life. But perhaps time is itself rooted in eternity and forms part of it? This is precisely the problem I should like to consider; I regard it as a fundamental problem of the metaphysics of history and one that constitutes an essential premiss for every interpretation of the historical process. We are forced to assume the existence of two kinds of time, a good and false, a true and untrue. On the one hand, there exists a false time; on the other, a deep time which forms part of eternity and which has escaped corruption. It is this problem which has opposed the various philosophical schools. One school, which has proved less dominant in the history of philosophical thought, but with which I am entirely in agreement, professes that just as it is possible to consider eternity in time, so it is to transcend closed time and transpose it into eternity on the condition, of course, that it evinces the eternal principle. Time therefore is not a finite circle into which nothing eternal can penetrate, but one that can be extended to comprehend it. This is one aspect of the problem. The other assumes that time itself is rooted in the depths of eternity. And thus what we call time in our world historical process, in our world reality, which is a process in time, is a sort of interior period, a sort of interior epoch in eternity itself. It denotes the existence not only of our terrestrial time within our terrestrial reality, but also that of a true celestial time in which the former is embedded and which it reflects and expresses; and, according to the ancient Gnostics, it denotes that of the aeons of the inmost depths of the Divine Being. But these aeons prove that time exists for the very foundations of being and that a certain time-process occurs in the latter; and that this process is not merely the form of our closed reality opposed to the deep reality which is apparently in no way related to time, but one that possesses its own celestial and divine time. And this would lead us to suppose that the very time-process itself, which is a world, historical process occurring in time and in our world of reality, has its origins in eternity.

A false distinction between time and eternity is the feature of a great many philosophical schools. It is the case, for example, of every phenomenalist conception whether it takes the form of Kantian criticism or that of English empiricism; for all phenomenalism considers that no direct means of communication between the world of reality manifested in time and the essence of being itself, between the phenomenon and the object itself, exists. These spheres and positions are incommensurable. They are inwardly divorced and there can be no question of their union. We live in a world that is manifest in time and that receives nothing directly from that deep and true reality which is not subject to the laws of time. Kant has developed a whole doctrine upon this basis which affirms that time and space are essentially transcendental forms of sensibility and of apprehension in which the knowable world is made manifest to us. Outwardly this world is manifest only in space and time. But its interior spiritual life is manifest only in time, since space does not constitute an interior form of spiritual reality. And similarly, neither time nor space forms can be transposed into the inmost core of being. It must be added that neither Platonism nor ancient Hindoo philosophy provide a tie between time and the inner essence of being. This latter is generally conceived as timeless and not as any process possessing its own time and epochs, in other words, as an immobile eternity opposed to any time process.

This conception of the relation existing between time and

[65]

eternity has left a deep impression upon the Christian consciousness, which tended to favour the view that the nature of time did not affect the depths of divine life. This, of course, is immediately connected with the problem whether the nature of movement and of process affects the divine life. My contention is in substance the same, though I approach the problem from the opposite side. I believe that to assert that time does not exist in the divine life is to approach the question exoterically without reaching the ultimate depths of gnosis. This exoteric standpoint, which has gained wide acceptance, and perhaps is the predominant one in the religious consciousness, holds that the divine life is not affected by the nature of history because human history is indissolubly bound up with time and cannot exist outside of it.

But if history postulates the existence of a false time, then the divine life ought to postulate that of a good and true time; one that is not opposed to eternity but represents some interior stage or epoch of eternity itself. For time, our world, the whole of our world process, from the moment of its inception to that of its end, represents a period, an aeon in the life of eternity, a period or an epoch rooted in it. This world process, therefore, is not shut off from all those deep forces which, though they may appear to us to be divine and mysterious, yet exercise their influence in it. They counteract that petrified consciousness for which the circle of our world reality is closed, and which does not admit the action of supernatural forces in our world process and its reciprocal influence in the supernatural world. I believe, therefore, that a real metaphysics of history can be built up only upon the basis of a dynamic and not a static interpretation of the nature of the world process.

The religious consciousness was not alone in thinking it necessary to shut off our world temporarily from the supernatural world. Both the positive-scientific consciousness and materialism, which is one of its offshoots, have affirmed the finality of our world and the non-existence of any other. Thus the whole essence of being is reduced in our consciousness to this temporal process. No other world exists: the circle of our reality is closed. A hermetic reality of this kind implies the denial of the existence of any other worlds. An open one, on the other hand, admits their existence. The metaphysics of history therefore must be based upon the fundamental hypothesis that the 'historical' is part of, and has its roots in, eternity. History is neither merely the scum of the world process nor the loss of all association with the roots of being; it forms a necessary part of eternity and of the drama that is fulfilled in it. History is the result of a deep interaction between eternity and time; it is the incessant eruption of eternity into time.

The historical character of Christianity may be attributed to the fact that the Christian consciousness had conceived eternity as manifesting and incarnating itself in time. The significance of Christianity as it manifests itself in the temporal and historical process lies in its demonstration that eternity or the divine reality can break the chain of time, penetrate into and appear as the dominant force in it. It postulates not only history but also time, without which it cannot exist. And yet it represents a constant struggle between the eternal and the temporal, a constant resistance of eternity to time, a constant effort of the eternal principle to achieve a victory over time. But the victory it seeks implies neither a departure from time, nor a denial of it, nor again the adoption of a

[67]

position detached from it. For this would imply the denial of history itself. It aims rather at the victory of eternity in the arena of time, that is, within the historical process itself. The struggle between eternity and time is the constant and tragic struggle between life and death; and it is conterminous with the historical process. The interaction and clash between the eternal and temporal principles is that between life and death, for the final sundering of time from eternity, a victory of the temporal over the eternal, would signify the triumph of death over life just as a final transition from the temporal to the eternal would mean a severance from the historical process. Thus a third approach, a third principle, exists which sums up the very essence of the struggle between the eternity of life and the mortality of time. It is the principle of founding the eternal upon the temporal.

The conception and interpretation of history as a complete whole postulates a goal, that is, the termination of this world aeon and stage of eternity which we call our world of reality and life. It implies the victory of the eternal principles over all that is corruptible, temporal or mortal, a victory in the most temporal of world realities over what Hegel called the false infinity. The latter does not admit a goal in time; it is an endless process which can achieve no final victory or solution. To conceive such an infinite process is to make the historical process meaningless, and its interpretation as a tragedy awaiting solution impossible. I shall dwell upon this further when considering the idea of progress and its connection with the teleology of history. In the meantime, we may postulate that historical time—that of our world of reality in which history occurs and of the aeon of man's terrestrial destiny—is present in eternity. And time assumes an ontological significance only because history itself is situated in eternity. The significance of the history taking place in this terrestrial aeon lies in its participation in the fulness of eternity, in that this aeon, emerging from its imperfect and defective state, should participate in the fulness of being peculiar to eternal life. This postulate of the metaphysics of history, based upon the relation of time and eternity, raises the essential problem, most closely connected with concrete history, of the relation between the past, the present and the future. If historical reality is intimately allied with time, if it is a process in time and a time-process postulating a special sort of ontological significance of time peculiar to being, the question arises of the relation existing between the past and the future. The time of our world reality and aeon is a divided and false time containing an evil and mortal principle; and it is, moreover, split up into the past, present and future.

In this connection we must consider St. Augustine's ingenious doctrine, according to which time is not only divided into sections, but each section of it is in revolt against the other. The future rebels against the past; and the past struggles against the destructive elements of the future. The historical process in time represents a constant, tragic and torturing struggle between these sections of time, between the past and the future. This cleavage is so strange and terrible that it finally transforms time into a sort of spectre or ghost; for, on analysis, we are driven to despair to find that the three sections of time, the past, the present and the future, are spectral and do not really exist. The present is an infinitely brief instant when the past has already ceased to exist and the future is not yet; it is a certain abstract point devoid of reality. The past is spectral because it has already ceased to exist. The future is spectral because it is not yet. Thus the thread of time is severed into three parts and no real time exists. This devouring of one section of time by another abolishes all reality and being in time. Time reveals an evil, deadly and destructive principle. For the death of the past hurried on by each consecutive instant and its plunge into the darkness of non-being, implied in every progress of time, are the very principles of death itself. The future is the murderer of every past instant. Thus false time is divided into past and future, between which lies a certain illusive point. The future devours the past in order to be transformed into a similar past, which in its turn is devoured by a succeeding past. This cleavage is a fundamental disease, defect and evil peculiar to the time of our world reality. To acknowledge only this evil and corrupt time would hinder the apprehension of the true historical reality which is attainable in some complete, true, undivided and immortal time and which fulfils itself in time, bearing life and not death. Our world time brings life only in a superficial way; in reality, it brings death because, in the process of creating life, it precipitates the past into the abyss of non-being. Thus every future must become past and must sooner or later fall under the dominion of this devouring torrent of the future. And there exists no true future which could comprehend the fulness of being, in which the true time could achieve a victory over false time, and in which the division could be transcended to permit integral time to become the eternal reality and the eternal to-day. And in that case the time of the present, in which everything occurs, and in which neither past nor future but only the true present exists, would be the only true time.

Let us examine more closely the nature of false time and

the history that occurs in it. Various schools of philosophy have freely contended that the future is reality and the past is less real than either the future or the present. But to admit even for a second that the past, that those severed parts which are cast off into eternity, have lost their reality, while only the present and the impending future constitute the true reality, is equivalent to denying that of history as belonging only to the past. The latter refers to that section of time which has to do with the past and in which everything 'future' is relegated to the 'past'. How then are we to account for the absorption into the past of the whole of historical reality, of all the great historical eras and the life of mankind with all their creating works and soul-inspiring epochs? Is all this reality or not? Is it sufficient to say that the past has been? That the history of the Jewish people, of ancient Egypt, of Greece, of Rome, of Christianity, of the Middle Ages, of the Renaissance, of the Reformation, and of the French Revolution was once a fact? Is it sufficient to assert that the whole of this past, which has become a part of history, is not essentially real but belongs to that true reality which is incommensurable with that of the yet unborn future? This point of view, however, is very widely current, and ultimately encourages the denial of the true reality of the 'historical'; for it favours an interpretation of history and its process of fulfilment which transforms everything into rapidly changing and ultimately spectral instants devoured by succeeding instants which all crumble away into the abyss of non-being of similar perishable instants.

The metaphysics of history ought to acknowledge the duration of history. For historical reality, which is considered to be a past reality, is in fact a true and lasting one. It is a reality which has neither disappeared nor perished, but which has become a part of a sort of eternal reality. It constitutes an interior stage and period of that eternal reality which has been relegated to the past and which is not conceived immediately like the present, because we live in a false, diseased and divided time. And this latter reflects the disintegration of our being. But we can live in the historical past as we live in the historical present and as we hope to live in the historical future. The integral life unites the three moments of the past, present and future in one. And thus historical reality is not dead, though it is relegated to the past; it is no less real than the current reality or that of the future which we cannot conceive, but which we only hope and expect. The past endures; but it depends upon the disintegration and limitations of our human existence and upon the fact that we do not live integrally in the past, that we are cut off from it and locked in the present instant between the past and the future, and that we regard the past as something remote. But the past is eternal reality. It is with its historical epochs an eternal reality in which each one of us in the depths of his spiritual experience achieves a victory over the corruption and disintegration of his being. Each one may commune with history to the extent in which he really exists in this aeon of world reality. The religious consciousness, indeed, cannot reconcile itself to the idea that anything truly living can die or disappear. Christianity is the greatest of religions because it is in the first place the religion of the Resurrection; and because it reconciles itself to neither death nor oblivion, but strives towards the resurrection of all that is truly existent.

We live in a world of historical reality, in a false and divided time, in which the past seems remote, the future yet unborn, and we are locked in the doubtful instant of the present. But what principle or force is directing the battle against this evil and mortal character of time? The battle of the eternal spirit without which the plot and unity of history, the succession of time and the division between the past, the present and the future, would become final and irreparable, because the loss of memory is, indeed, the chief and fundamental sign of insanity. Memory is the principle which conducts a constant battle against the mortal principle of time. It battles in the name of eternity against the mortal dominion of time. It is the fundamental way of conceiving the reality of the past in our false time wherein it endures only by means of memory. The historical memory is the greatest manifestation of the eternal spirit in our temporal reality. It upholds the historical connection of the times. It is the very foundation of history. Without it history would not exist; for even if history did fulfil itself, the cleavage between the past, the present and the future would be so hopeless as to render all apprehension of history impossible. All historical knowledge is but a remembrance, one or another form of the triumph of memory over the spirit of corruption. By means of memory we resurrect the remote past which had seemingly perished or been engulfed in some dark abyss. Memory is therefore the eternal ontological basis of all history. It conserves the paternal principle, our relationship with our fathers; for the latter is synonymous with that between the past, present and future. To forget our descent completely would be to forget the past. And this would be equivalent to a state of insanity in which mankind would live only upon the rags of time, in its torn instants without any co-ordinating principle.

[73]

Thus the Futurist interpretation of life, which is based upon the cult of the future and that of every present moment, indicates real insanity on the part of mankind. It renounces all ties, that is, all co-ordination of memory and even the possibility of such a thing. The historical process has a double nature: it both conserves and annihilates. On the one hand, it symbolizes the union of the past and future; and on the other, a cleavage with the past. It is in fact both conservative and revolutionary. And history is founded upon the interaction of these two principles. The action of one of these principles only would produce a real disintegration of the times; for the fulfilment of history is based not only on the conservation of the tie between the present, the future and the past, but also on the continuation of the past in the future. Thus the great riches of the past help to prevent us from impoverishing ourselves, and we still preserve the means of enriching ourselves by the creative future.

The co-operation of these two principles is essential to the historical process, which is by its nature such a tie and complex fulfilment. A true and non-disintegrated time, one that knows no cleavage between the past and future, a noumenal and not a phenomenal time, is also operative in history which is assailed by a false, devouring and annihilating time; and this latter transforms our life into a cemetery where the sons, oblivious of their fathers, build up their new life upon the bones of their ancestors. The establishment therefore of a proper relationship between the past and the future is all-important for a true historical consciousness. The exclusive cult of the future at the expense of the past, which is the feature of the various theories of progress, makes life subservient to a disruptive and deadly principle destructive of all co-ordination and of the integral reality of time. Subservience to the deadly power of time hinders the apprehension of the significance of human destiny as a celestial destiny. A false time brings about a cleavage between the metaphysical and the historical, while the metaphysical origins of history ought, on the contrary, to establish a tie between them. The cleavage between the eternal and the temporal is both the greatest delusion of consciousness and an obstacle to the foundation of a true philosophy of history.

I shall now consider the last fundamental postulate of the metaphysics of history. All that I have been saying has a direct bearing upon the religious postulate of history. The acceptance of the principle of the freedom of evil inherent in history constitutes this fundamental postulate without which history cannot be comprehended. The principle of true freedom also implies the acceptance of that of the freedom of evil. Without it the historical process can be understood in time only in terms of established institutions, but the metaphysics and the ultimate depths of history remain impenetrable. Ancient myths and traditions, however, make it easier to grasp the inner essence of history. They teach us that the principle of the freedom of evil is inherent in the universal historical process.

Two fundamental positions can, indeed, be defended if we accept man's destiny to be the main theme of the metaphysics of history. Firstly, there is the evolutionary point of view which dominated the nineteenth century, and which held that man was the product of world forces and that he had, through evolution, ascended in the historical process. Man was both the child of the world and the product of processes of development from lower states. Thus man, emerging through evolution from animal and half-animal states, gradually perfects himself and, becoming truly himself, then ascends to still higher states.

The second position is that which had apparently been superseded by the scientific theories of the nineteenth and twentieth centuries, and which maintained that man's Fall and certain acts of sin and divorce from the sources of divine life and higher truth preceded the evolutionary, secondary and partial processes in man's destiny. This belief lies at the foundation of the traditions and myths about the Original Sin, those of the Bible and of the Christian and many other forms of religious consciousness. For Christianity it is more natural to admit man's Fall and alienation from the true sources of life, after which his destiny is accomplished in the world. The scientific standpoint, on the other hand, precludes the identification of man's destiny with that of the world and his predetermination by it. Nor does it admit the existence of such a pre-world man. In its logical development, the purely evolutionary doctrine denies that man's destiny can be the theme of history. Let us admit that a process of evolution does take place, that man ascends from the lower states to man's estate, and that he perfects himself still further along a straight line of development determined by world forces of which he is the child. This does not imply the acceptance of man's destiny as the theme of the metaphysics of history. For, to admit the manifestation of man's destiny in world history, it is also necessary to admit his pre-world existence; that his destiny originated and was determined prior to the establishment of that world of reality where occur all those processes of evolution and development by which the evolutionary theory tries to explain both man's origins and his further development. Such a view can only prove the negation of human destiny, which postulates the existence of a primary human nature created by the higher divine nature and suffering its tragic destiny in the world. It presupposes, too, the action of pre-world forces upon man who relies upon these interior sources for the fulfilment of his destiny. Without this one cannot speak of destiny in the real sense of the word; for it can exist only if man is the child of God and not of the world.

This constitutes the real religious-metaphysical postulate of the metaphysics of history. Man is the child of God and suffers a tragic destiny in a world that is subject to decadence as well as development. At the foundations of this destiny lies the original freedom with which God's child has been endowed and which is the true reflection and image of the Creator. This freedom has become the source of man's tragic destiny, and that of history with all its conflicts and horrors. Freedom by its nature presupposes that of evil as well as of good. There would be no movement in the world if only the freedom of God and of good were to predetermine human destiny. The world and historical processes are based upon the freedom of good and evil, that of renouncing as well as of communing with the source of higher divine life. The freedom of evil, indeed, forms the real foundation of history. And the ancient tale of Man's Fall, that of Adam and Eve, which epitomizes what must have happened in the history of being prior to the origin of the world process, is an account of primordial history, of that which lay beyond the boundaries dividing off our time from eternity. This primordial act, which is recorded in ancient myths and traditions, took place not in the realms of our time but in those of eternity

[77]

where it originated. It helped to engender our false time, that evil inherent in our time which is associated with the disintegration of the unique and complete time into the past, present and future. Man's highest dignity and freedom lie in the consciousness of his higher primordial origin; and that, too, of his destiny which later came to be governed by the action of complex world forces. Science, with its evolutionary theories, of course, devoted its attention solely to the latter. I do not mean to imply that the whole of the evolutionary doctrine is false; but only that it has a different interior significance.

The evolutionary theory contains a great deal that is true concerning man's origin and destiny in the world. But it is preoccupied with secondary and not primary processes; it has no light to throw on those deeper sources, which preceded the birth of our world of reality and of our time, and on those processes of which religious traditions speak and which only metaphysical knowledge can apprehend. The result, however, is not a clash between these two standpoints, but the interpretation of one in the light of the other. The influence of environment, which the evolutionary theory studies, is true only of man's secondary destiny in our world which we, on the other hand, explain in terms of certain events that occurred prior to the birth of our world reality in some deeper and primordial reality. Only then can the history of mankind be understood as a free trial of human spiritual forces and as the expiation of man's Original Sin and Fall which were brought about through the agency of the freedom, inherent in him. Human destiny within the confines of history is illuminated by the greatest significance of this freedom, which predetermines the course of human destiny in temporal reality. It demonstrates that within the confines of history all compulsion and unfree fulfilment of the highest Divine Will and the highest Divine Truth are unnecessary to God, Who must deny any perfection of man that is the result of the process of either necessity or compulsion.

All that is unfree is undesirable to God. We might, indeed, echo the words of the Grand Inquisitor, when he reproaches Christ, but re-interpret them in praise as the greatest religious statement of truth concerning the essence of human existence. The Grand Inquisitor said: 'You have desired man's free gift of love and that he should follow You of his free will, tempted and made captive by You.' Freedom is in its essence the principle of tragedy, of tragic dualism and of the antithesis inherent in primal freedom which alone makes possible such a tragic destiny. We tend to think in terms of a process of development or disintegration and not in those of destiny in the real sense of the word. Destiny depends on freedom; that is the greatest confession of the Christian world distinguishing it from the ancient world which ignored such a conception. This is obvious from the structure of the ancient tragedy which was founded upon fate. The ancient pagan world has only an obscure presentiment of freedom. The Christian consciousness, however, introduces a radical change. It associates human destiny with original freedom. It may, indeed, be affirmed that the Christian consciousness alone conceived the idea of a Providence, which is inherent in the structure of St. Augustine's philosophy of history. Providence is neither necessity nor compulsion; it is the antinomous union of God's Will and human freedom.

What is the origin of man's historical destiny when considered from the standpoint of this ancient tradition of man's original freedom and therefore of his Original Fall? In our world of reality and time man's historical destiny begins with his immersion in the depths of nature, that is, according to theosophical terminology, with involution. Man's immersion in nature was the immediate result of his Fall and free repudiation of the divine sources of life, which was followed by the loss of freedom and its transformation into a certain interior necessity and compulsion. Original evil gives rise to its physical destiny in nature, which is the domain investigated by biology, anthropology and sociology. Man's destiny, when immersed in nature, is not that of a child of God, of a free spirit created in the image and likeness of Him, but that of a natural being and child of the world. Man has always been and still remains a dual being participating in two worlds: in the highest divine and free world whose image he is and in the natural world in which he is immersed. He shares the destiny of the latter, which reacts upon him and ties him hand and foot, so that his consciousness becomes obscured and his higher origin and participation in the highest spiritual reality are forgotten. Man's dependence on nature, his immersion in natural necessity, his divorce from the highest divine reality which endowed him with freedom and, finally, his existence in another and natural reality where necessity sets the stamp of its law upon him; all these are reflected in the first stages of human history, in mythology and the processes of its consciousness.

Schelling has an ingenious theory according to which mythology represents the repetition in the human spirit and consciousness of the processes of nature. The human consciousness reflects and repeats the historical and cosmogonic processes of nature, which take the form of mythology in its primal stages. The mythological consciousness is thus full of cosmic myths in which man is revealed as a natural being related to the spirits of nature. These myths also disclose the ties uniting man with the primary processes of world creation and formation, which go back much further than the consolidation of matter from which science, later, dates its study of world evolution. Deep natural processes were at work even before the consolidation of matter; and man's destiny was still rooted in them, although his divorce from the higher spiritual sources had already taken place. Man's original prehistory may therefore be regarded as a certain religious mythological process.

Mythology is the original source of human history. It is the opening page of a tale about man's terrestrial destiny, which succeeded his celestial one and the prologue which was enacted in heaven. The prologue, which had proclaimed man's intimate relation with God and his freedom and Fall, is followed by the next act in the natural world in the form of a mythological process. This is the second act in eternity but the first in man's terrestrial history. Certain moments still partaking of eternity are to be apprehended in the uttermost depths and the initial stages of time in which man's primordial destiny was fulfilled, and he first suffered his Fall and came upon the sharp division of our reality from eternity. It is only later, in another time, that our world aeon begins to consolidate, close and set itself up as an antithesis to eternity. And then, what we have termed the celestial eternity moves away into transcendental space which appears to be excluded from our world. But the earlier religious myths and traditions offer no sharp demarcation between eternity and time; and this constitutes one of the greatest difficulties in the way of apprehending ancient religious life. Our consciousness has become so accustomed to our world reality, its confinement and the boundaries dividing off terrestrial reality from eternity and true time, that we often find it very difficult to break through its crust and to reach that primal state at the dawn of human consciousness in which no such divisions existed.

No such demarcation is to be found in the Bible or in early religious traditions and myths. And that is one of the reasons why we find it so difficult to understand the interwoven history of earth and heaven, of time and eternity. The action apparently unfolds itself on our planet, in our time and reality; but it also seems to be taking place in another time and world which had preceded the origin of our world aeon. The historical information provided by the Bible had been regarded before the advent of modern science as scientific knowledge in the spheres of history, geography, geology and anthropology. The further developments of philosophy and the sciences tended to discredit the naive teaching of the Bible, which lost its authority in these spheres. I do not mean to imply that scientific criticism can affect to any extent the religious truth contained in Biblical traditions. For, after all, the religious truth of myths and traditions is not limited to the material they provide for the natural or historical sciences. Nor, again, is it confined to any authority they may claim in the sphere of contemporary history, geology, or biology. It lies rather in the symbolic revelation they offer of the deep processes operative beyond the boundaries dividing off the time of our aeon from that of eternal reality. Scientific and philosophical criticism cannot be wholly based upon such revelations. Therefore in so far as the ecclesiastical con-

[82]

sciousness had attempted to impose religion as a compulsory science, it adopted a hostile attitude to science and, in this way, disarmed religious truth. But it ought to be clear to the religious and philosophical consciousness that these spheres may be demarcated.

The religious content of the ancient traditions and myths does not constitute a science or objective knowledge. Nor can it compete with the latter. But it does represent the revelation of far deeper truths bearing upon quite different spheres. The great truth of the Bible, which provides the point of intersection, the meeting point of terrestrial and celestial history, the origins of man's terrestrial and celestial destinies, ought to be approached both philosophically and religiously in the light of the New and not the Old Testament. It is true that the interpretation of the Bible according to the Old Testament has been predominant in Christianity itself. Thus the whole of the Biblical cosmology and anthropology tends to be reduced to the limits of man's consciousness in the Old Testament. The limits within which truth was revealed to man in the Old Testament have left their imprint upon the Bible. Its revelation was therefore refracted within certain human limits and was passed on in this form to the higher stages of spiritual consciousness. The ecclesiastical attitude to Biblical truths tends to accept those limits of revelation peculiar to man's ancient nature, the destiny of the Jewish people and of those with whom it was indissolubly bound. This had its effect upon the Christian consciousness of the New Testament and imposed certain limitations upon it. Thus Christian anthropology and cosmology, the doctrine of man's origin, all display in their most predominant form the stamp of the limitations peculiar to

[83]

man in the Old Testament. These limitations are like-wise apparent in Christian dogma and its metaphysics of history, since they are founded upon the limited Biblical anthropological and cosmological doctrines. The consciousness of the Old Testament is therefore an obstacle to the foundation of a true metaphysics of history, for the latter according to its fundamental premiss ought to break through the limitations of man's ancient consciousness which Christianity failed to overcome. And thus the metaphysical consciousness of the Old Adam continues to set up its barriers in the New Testament period of human history. It also influenced the structure of the metaphysics of history.

A change and transformation of man's interior history was imperative in the light of the New Testament, of the New Adam and of the new man, who had thrown off the yoke of natural necessity and the wrath of God. It had been impossible to meet God because it was believed that such a meeting would prove man's annihilation. The following elements therefore constitute man's fundamental destiny throughout Christian history: the Old Testament feeling for God and nature; the fear of God's wrath, which man experienced after his Fall to a lower plane of natural life; the transcending of this feeling through the New Testament revelation of the New Adam which makes God endlessly near to man; and, finally, the New Testament feeling of liberation from the spirits and demons of nature who tormented man in the ancient world. This inner spiritual change is what distinguishes the whole of Christian history from that of the pagan and Biblical world. As a result, man began to liberate himself inwardly, on the one hand, from the power of the natural demons through the mystery of Redemption and, on the other, from the Jewish subservience to God as a remote, menacing and wrathful power which it was terrifying and dangerous for man to meet. The whole of Christian as well as ancient and Biblical history may now be conceived in the light of the new revelation and the new human nature which it produced.

The Christian consciousness has so far but inadequately applied this process of revaluation. It is true to say that the new revelation of Biblical truth was the contribution rather of great individual mystics such as Jacob Boehme in his *Mysterium Magnum* than that of Christian philosophy in general. The new revelation, however, constitutes a corner stone of the philosophy of history. For the world process now comes under the sign of the New Adam or Christ; and this fact of the revelation of a new human nature is all-important for the philosophy of history. It inaugurates an entirely new era in the interpretation of the essence and meaning of history. Man's celestial history is now brought to an end and he enters upon his terrestrial history and destiny. The philosophy of man's terrestrial destiny may be said to begin with the philosophy of history and destiny of the Jewish people. Here lies the axis of world history. The theme provided by the destiny of the Jewish people fulfils itself throughout the whole course of world history.

CHAPTER V

THE DESTINY OF THE JEWS

The Jews played a decisive rôle in the formation of the historical consciousness. They were the first to introduce the principles of the 'historical' and a keen feeling for historical destiny into the life of mankind. I now propose to examine their destiny, its significance in relation to world history and its influence as an ineradicable and universal principle of specific function. The Jews have played an all-important rôle in history. They are pre-eminently an historical people and their destiny reflects the indestructibility of the divine decrees.

Their destiny is too imbued with the 'metaphysical' to be explained either in material or positive-historical terms. Moreover, it presents no sign of that antithesis between the metaphysical and the historical, which I regard as an obstacle to the apprehension of the inner significance of history. I remember how the materialist interpretation of history, when I attempted in my youth to verify it by applying it to the destinies of peoples, broke down in the case of the Jews, where destiny seemed absolutely inexplicable from the materialistic standpoint. And, indeed, according to the materialistic and positivist criterion, this people ought long ago to have perished. Its survival is a mysterious and wonderful phenomenon demonstrating that the life of this people is governed by a special predetermination, transcending the processes of adaptation expounded by the materialistic interpretation of history. The survival of the Jews, their resistance to destruction, their endurance under absolutely peculiar conditions and the fateful rôle played by them in history; all these point to the particular and mysterious foundations of their destiny.

The history of the Jews is not only a phenomenon; it is also a noumenon in that special sense of the word to which I drew attention when speaking of the phenomenal-noumenal historical antithesis. I said that the historical not only represented man's external relations, but that it might also reveal the very noumenon and essence of his being. The peculiarity of Jewish destiny consists in its incommensurability with either the pre-Christian or the Christian era. Scientific criticism applied to traditional Biblical history can neither discredit the universal rôle played by the Jews nor offer a satisfactory explanation of their mysterious destiny. Nor does this criticism grapple with the absolutely peculiar tie existing between the Jews and the 'historical', and their extraordinarily intense feeling for history.

The Jewish destiny is characterized by a particularly dramatic intensity which makes the purely Aryan spirit seem dull by comparison. Whatever the contributions of the Greek or the Hindoo spirits, perhaps superior in many ways to that of the Jews, their non-historical nature is apparent. They do not carry the revelation of historical destiny, of its drama, of the intensity of historical action and movement. India offers the example of a very ancient and essentially non-historical culture, which has stopped still in the depths of its interior spiritual contemplations without as yet venturing to participate directly in the dramatic action of universal history. The same in another sense is true of Greece. There the

Aryan spirit achieved an aesthetic and philosophy that have not been surpassed by any culture in the world. But this spirit manifested itself in a static cosmos closed to all tension of historical action.

How are we to explain this fact? The 'historical' possesses a religious foundation, rests on one or another form of religious consciousness. This is the basic premiss we have to consider. The religious nature of the Jewish spirit contained a principle which was to determine its intensely historical character and destiny. A comparison between the Jewish religion and that of other pre-Christian pagan peoples confirms the contention that Jewish history represented the revelation of God in the historical destiny of humanity, while that of other pagan peoples represented the revelation of God in nature. This distinction between the foundations of the Jewish and the pagan Aryan religions helps us to establish the historical character of the Jewish people.

Jewish religion is permeated with the messianic idea which is, indeed, its pivot. Israel lived in expectation of the Day of Judgment when it would abandon the sorrowful historical destiny which was the lot of its people, to enter upon a sort of all-illuminating world era. The messianic idea is the determining factor in the historical drama of the Jewish people. The expectation of the future Messiah and the passionate longing for His coming gave rise to that dualism in the Jewish religious consciousness which bound the destiny of the Jewish people to that of mankind. This dualism of the messianic consciousness aspired towards an historical progression and fulfilment.

The Jewish spirit constitutes a distinct racial type; and it preserved in the nineteenth and twentieth centuries the fun-

[88]

damental peculiarities of the spirit of ancient Israel. The destiny of the latter continues to be reflected in the different stages of the historical life and destiny of contemporary Jews. Their spirit, although based upon that of the Ancient Hebrews, evolves in the nineteenth and twentieth centuries a distorted and perverted form of Messianism, that which expects the coming of another Messiah following the repudiation of the true one. It is still animated by the aspiration towards the future, by the stubborn and persistent demand that the future should bring with it an all-resolving principle, an all-resolving truth and justice on earth, in the name of which the Jewish people is prepared to declare war on all historical traditions, sacraments and associations. The Jewish people is by its nature an historical people, active and self-willed, but not possessed of that power of contemplation which is peculiar to the highest levels of Aryan spiritual life. Karl Marx, a very typical Jew, was still striving quite late in history to resolve the ancient Biblical precept of 'earn thy bread in the sweat of thy brow'. Marxian Socialism, emerging from an entirely new historical background, reiterates the demand for earthly bliss. It is true that, superficially, the Marxist doctrine breaks away from the Jewish religious traditions and rebels against every sacred principle; but in reality the messianic idea of the Jews as God's chosen people is transferred to a class, namely the proletariat. The working class now becomes the new Israel, God's chosen people, destined to emancipate and save the world. All the characteristics of Jewish Messianism are applied to this class. The same drama, passion and impatience which had characterized Israel, the people of God, are here manifest. The Jewish people had always been God's people, a people endowed with a tragic historical des-

[89]

tiny. Before its God had been recognized as the unique God, Creator of the universe and Lord of all, He had been the God of the race, a national Deity. This association of the mono-theistic idea with the national destiny of God's chosen people was the factor that determined all the peculiarities and the specific characteristics of the religious destiny of the Jews.

This brings us to one of the aspects of the Jewish religious consciousness which particularly distinguishes it from the Aryan, and which exercised a determining influence in the history of the Jewish people. The Jews apprehended God transcendentally; they conceived a tremendous gulf between Him and man; and this made a face to face meeting with Him impossible without danger of death. The Semite looked up from below at God in His infinite height. But this remote-ness from and awe of God, this transcendental consciousness of Him as within and above man, was of great moment in the birth of the historical drama. It set history in motion; and made for the sense of a dramatic relationship between man, the people and a transcendental God, and an encounter between the people and God on the highway of history. The typical Aryan consciousness of God, which attains its purest state in the ancient Hindoo religion, is an immanent one; it is an apprehension of God in the ultimate depths of man himself. But such a consciousness is not particularly favourable to his-torical movement. It elaborates a contemplative insight into the depths of being that is antithetical to the religious life which creates exterior historical movement. This latter, on the other hand, was favoured by the principles behind the Jewish reli-gious consciousness, and also by the concrete idea of God as a personal God who entertained personal relations with man. Indeed, this idea formed the foundation of Jewish national history. The historical character of such a relationship between man and God, between the people and God, derived from the exterior drama of the situation.

The Jewish people in their primitive conception of life were obsessed by the passionate idea of justice and its terrestrial fulfilment. I believe that this other specific idea of the Jewish people, this demand for justice to be realized on earth together with this aspiration towards the future, predetermined the whole complexity of Jewish historical destiny. The Greeks, who were typical Aryans, had never been obsessed by the idea of justice. If it was not absolutely foreign to the Hellenic spirit, at least it was never more than a minor preoccupation.

The idea of justice was very closely related to the problem of the individuality and the immortality of the soul. The Greeks, more than any other people, had helped to work out the idea of the immortality of the psyche or the soul. But this conception was foreign to the Jews, for whom the centre of gravity lay not so much in man's individual destiny as in that of the people as a whole. The Jewish religious consciousness was remarkable for its freedom from the idea of an immortal soul, which makes its appearance only in the very last stage of Jewish history immediately before the advent of Christianity. The Jews, indeed, were very late in arriving at the idea of personal immortality. In their conception of the relationship between God and man, God alone is immortal. To the Jewish consciousness the idea of man's immortality seemed to imply an exaggeration of man's significance. It only allowed the immortality of the people.

Renan, that brilliant but not profound writer, highly endowed with psychological insight but deficient in religious

[91]

imagination, sums up excellently the characteristics of the Jews in his *History of the Jewish People*. This is perhaps his most interesting work, though it is marred by certain exaggerations and an insufficient comprehension of the Jewish destiny. In it, however, he very cogently remarks: 'The ancient Semite repudiated as chimerical all those forms in which other peoples imagined their after-life. Only God was eternal; man lived but a span of years; an immortal man would be God. Man could only prolong his ephemeral existence for a short while in his children.' I believe,—and for me this constitutes the key to the whole historical destiny of the Jewish people,—that the Jewish consciousness represents the union of the aspiration to realize justice and truth on earth with that which seeks to achieve individual immortality.

The dualism inherent in the Jewish messianic consciousness determined the fateful destiny of the Jews in so far as it combined the expectation of the true Messiah, the Son of God, Who was to appear among the Jews, and that of the false Messiah, or Antichrist. As a result of this dualism the Jewish people, with the exception of a chosen few made up of the Apostles and a few early Christians, did not recognize the true Messiah. They failed to recognize and repudiated the Messiah in Christ. This is the central event in world history, the event towards which history had been moving and from which it has since proceeded; the event which makes of the Jews, as it were, the axis of universal history. For it was they who discovered and expounded the problem which universal Christian history attempts to solve. At the same time we may observe, along with a religiously justifiable principle animating this intense Jewish striving after truth, justice and happiness on earth, an unwarrantable principle of conflict with

God, an unwillingness to accept the Will of God. There is a resistance to God, an arbitrary assertion of a purely human justice and truth and their fulfilment on earth against that destiny of all mankind revealed in the life and history of the world according to God's inscrutable will and design. And there is a tendency to transfer the vital principle to the surface of our planet in the apparent absence of a life that is eternal and immortal. This is equivalent to denying man's immortality and the everlasting life which contains and fulfils the meaning of human destiny.

But human destiny, whose pains and torments can in no wise be redeemed within the narrow limits of a single life, finds its fulfilment in another life; and this fulfilment transcends the logic and justice of man's limited rational and ethical nature. The Jewish people was not content to demand and expect a messianic fulfilment in history and a victory over falsehood. They also adopted a popular pretension which challenged Providence and contradicted the essential notion of an immortal life. This was the idea that everything must find its fulfilment and solution in this mortal and terrestrial life. According to this idea justice must be realized in this world at any cost. As Renan has well said: 'The Jewish thinker, like the contemporary nihilist, was of the opinion that the world had no justification if justice were not feasible in it.'

The Book of Job is one of the most astounding in the Bible. The interior ethical dialectic revealed in the Bible is based upon the assumption that a just man ought to be rewarded by a happy life on earth. Therefore the undeserved calamities that befall Job provoke in him a profound ethical-religious crisis. Job's destiny is considered without any reference to the idea of immortality and eternal life, where his sufferings might be transcended. For Job truth and justice must be finally fulfilled in his terrestrial life, since they cannot hope to be fulfilled anywhere else. The idea of a reward or punishment in some other life does not enter into the religious hypothesis of this Book. Thus the dialectic of one of the greatest and most fundamental themes of the human spirit is developed on a purely terrestrial plane. It is that the just may suffer on earth while the sinners and the wicked may flourish and rejoice. This is the eternal theme handed down from age to age and reflected in some of the greatest creations of the human spirit. This theme, as expressed by the Jewish religious consciousness, suffered from the limitations imposed upon it by the inability to situate man's destiny in the perspective of eternal life. This limitation helps to explain the intensity peculiar to the Jewish people in their historical life on earth; for the destiny of the individual as of the people was not considered in the perspective of eternal life, but only in that of their historical life on earth.

The Jews infused great energy into their historical life and endowed it with a religious significance. The Aryan peoples, on the other hand, were preoccupied with the problem of individual destiny. The Aryan found it difficult to consider the idea of a historical destiny on earth. Their consciousness in this life was concerned with attaining to the contemplation of eternal life. To them the historical destiny of mankind appeared devoid of interest when compared with the contemplation of other spiritual worlds. The Greeks, even at the height of their spiritual life, had no religious consciousness of the significance of man's historical destiny on earth. It has no place in Plato's philosophy, which was one of the greatest ex-

[94]

pressions of the Greek spirit. Plato was concerned with the original forms of being and with the world of ideas in which he recognized the primal static reality. He was unable to detach himself from this in order to consider the mobile empirical world and its implicit exposition of the historical process. And here we reach the frontiers of the Hellenic religious consciousness.

The antithesis established between the historical immortality of the people, on the one hand, and individual immortality, on the other, is characteristic of the whole destiny of the Jewish people. Even the prophets who announced the Christian dispensation had no conception of immortality. The Jewish religion had no place for either mythology, mystery or metaphysics in the true sense of the word. The German Jewish philosopher Cohen, who belonged to the Neo-Kantian School, went back in the last period of his work to religious sources and began to advocate an original Jewish modernism purified by critical and philosophical reason. Cohen affirms that his religion is a prophetic one, essentially future in reference, whereas every mythological religion is indissolubly associated with the past. A myth always tells a story about the past. The prophetic character of the Jewish religious consciousness, which elevates it above all others, also explains its freedom from mythological elements. Cohen claims that this prophetic character makes Jewish religion pre-eminently ethical, and expounds it according to the Kantian philosophy. But he overlooks the fact that Judaism does contain a myth, —the eschatological myth which is admittedly concerned with the future and not the past. It forms the mystical foundation of the Jewish people and its history, and is peculiar to the Jewish consciousness.

[95]

The word myth, of course, possesses for me a real significance and is not in any way opposed to reality. This peculiarity of the Jewish consciousness helps to explain the Judaic origins of Socialism as a definite universal historical principle. Socialism is not a phenomenon peculiar to our time, although it has in our day acquired an extraordinary force and unprecedented influence over the entire historical field. It is one of the universal historical principles. These latter, however, have their roots in the remotest ages and, like all ancient principles, are constantly active and in conflict with their opposites. I believe that Socialism is based upon a Jewish religious principle, upon the eschatological myth and the profound dualism of the Jewish consciousness, which has proved to be tragic not only for the history of the Jews themselves but for that of all mankind. This dualism of the Jewish historical consciousness gave rise to the religious millennium which aspired towards the future in a passionate demand and longing for the fulfilment of the millenary Kingdom of God on earth, and the advent of the Day of Judgment when evil would finally be vanquished by good, and when an end would come to the injustice and sufferings common to the terrestrial destiny of mankind. This millenarianism is the original source of the religiously tainted Socialism.[1]

This can further be explained by the fact that Judaism is by its spiritual nature collective, whereas Aryanism tends to be individual. The alliance of the Jewish spirit with the destiny of the people, the inability to conceive individual destiny apart from the existence of the people or the destiny of Israel,

[1]A distinction must be made between Socialism as a religion and as a practical social movement defending labour and workers against capitalism. The second aspect is by far the more authentic.

the transference of the centre of gravity to an historical and impersonal national life, all make of the Jews a collective people. The Aryan spirit and culture, on the other hand, discovered for the first time the individual principle and exalted the individual spirit. The idea of both individual freedom and the sense of individual guilt were foreign to the Jewish spirit. For it the idea of freedom could only apply to the people; and its natural collectivism conceived guilt as the collective responsibility of the people before God. The demand that truth should be victorious at any cost on earth, the longing for truth and victory, for truth and justice, in the collective destiny of the people; all these formed the leading motive and spiritual principle behind the tragedy of Christ's repudiation by the Jewish people.

Renan, with his usual partiality in this matter, establishes a keen distinction between the Aryan and the Semitic types. According to him, 'The Aryan, who begins by admitting that the gods are unjust, does not experience the same passionate desire for earthly bliss. Allured by the chimera of an after-life (only such a chimera can inspire great deeds), he does not take the pleasures of life seriously; he builds his house for eternity. The Semite, on the other hand, builds his house for earthly enjoyment; he has no desire to wait; the fame or happiness which he does not experience does not exist for him. A Semite believes too much in God; the Aryan too much in the eternity of man. The Semite has given us God; the Aryan the immortality of the soul.'

This definition is very one-sided and does not correspond to the complex historical reality. But it contains a certain element of truth and it explains the peculiar intensity of the Jewish messianic expectation of the advent of the beatific

Kingdom of God on earth. It reveals, too, the predetermining dualism of Jewish Messianism. Let us consider the following passage from the Book of Isaiah. We shall be astonished to find that it can be interpreted in two ways: as the source of a real expectation of a terrestrial Kingdom and as that of a divine messianic feast. This is the passage: 'The wolf also shall dwell with the lamb, and the leopard shall lie down with the kid; and the calf and the young lion and the fatling together; and a little child shall lead them. And the cow and the bear shall feed; their young ones shall lie down together: and the lion shall eat straw like the ox. And the suckling child shall play on the hole of the asp, and the weaned child shall put his hand on the cockatrice' den. They shall not hurt nor destroy in all my holy mountain: for the earth shall be full of the knowledge of the Lord, as the waters cover the sea.'

No other people in the world was ever so obsessed by the messianic expectation of the advent of beatitude, of God's truth and Kingdom. It is true that there was another and aesthetical aspect to this messianic consciousness. It could also transform itself into the expectation of the Messiah as a terrestrial king who would realize the Kingdom, the national Kingdom of Israel, on earth, and thereby ultimate felicity. Jewish apocalypticism is full of such interpretations of the messianic consciousness. Renan says elsewhere: 'The true Israelite is torn with discontent and obsessed by an unquenchable thirst for the future.' This unquenchable thirst is the thirst for the advent sooner or later of the Kingdom of God on earth. Renan also says: 'The Jew, unlike the Christian, is incapable of submitting himself to Providence. Poverty and humiliation are considered a virtue by the Christian; but the

Jew regards them as a misfortune which must be combated. Abuse and violence are borne meekly by the Christian, but they revolt the Jew.'

This definition helps us to establish the distinction between the Jewish and the Christian consciousness. The latter proves altogether unacceptable to those Jews who have preserved their Hebrew characteristics. It also helps us to explain the revolutionary nature of the Jewish religious consciousness. The Jew easily becomes a revolutionary. For the Jews have always upheld the myth that history is founded upon the exploitation of man by man. I do not mean this in the narrow contemporary sense of the word, but in one that defines the character of a type; I mean it in the sense in which the Jews have defied destiny and the experiences and sufferings that go with it; in the sense in which they have persistently and passionately demanded the fulfilment of truth and happiness on earth. The idea of a terrestrial kingdom was to them not a worldly or secular idea, but a religious and theocratic one. This was largely due to the fact that they had but a comparatively vague notion of the temporal state in general and of a secular state in particular. Here we meet with an apparent contradiction. For while no people ever thirsted so passionately for the realization of their national terrestrial kingdom, the Jews found themselves, in fact, deprived in their historical destiny on earth of that elementary prerogative which all other peoples possessed. The Jews were indeed denied the possibility of existing as an independent state. The passionate desire to realize their terrestrial kingdom had ultimately produced the opposite result, namely, that the Jews were denied the common heritage of all those other peoples, whose thirst for the realization of a kingdom on earth was so much less.

This is, indeed, one of the paradoxes of Jewish destiny, most intimately bound up with Jewish Messianism.

The spiritual life of the Hebrew people was destined to culminate in the Coming of Christ and in His Crucifixion. Christ, however, did not fulfil its expectations of an earthly ruler who would realize the terrestrial kingdom of Israel. This fact gave rise to a profound contradiction in the destiny of the Jewish people. For, by repudiating the Crucifixion, it found itself virtually crucified in its own destiny. This constitutes the fundamental antithesis pervading the Jewish religious destiny. The passionate speculation of the Jewish people with regard to its terrestrial kingdom underlies the passionate striving of modern times to realize a Socialist kingdom on earth,—one that is reserved for no one people in particular, but for mankind in general. The fulfilment of this Socialist paradise was to be brought about not by the Messiah but by a messianic class,—the proletariat. But this passionate concern for man's terrestrial and historical destiny, which is the fundamental peculiarity of the Jewish spirit, contradicts the expectations of an immortal life in that the fulfilment of the highest divine truth is not extended to the sublime plane of immortality. He who believes in immortality ought to look soberly on terrestrial life and realize that it is impossible to achieve a conclusive victory on earth over the dark irrational principle; and that sufferings, evil and imperfections are the inevitable lot of man. But although the Jewish people had attained to a very high religious level, although it achieved the Christian position, yet its sense of immortality was much fainter than that of either the Persians or the Egyptians. The former, who were a great Aryan people of the East, had intuitions of true faith in immortality and the Resurrection;

the latter, too, longed passionately for the Resurrection of the dead, and the whole of Egyptian history was founded upon this longing. The pyramids constitute a great monument to the human spirit and refute the materialistic conception of history and interpretation of life.[1]

In the course of its further historical destiny the Jewish people too came to believe in immortality and the Resurrection. It had trodden the path pursued by other peoples before the advent of Christianity. The Jewish people was monotheistic and had an overwhelming feeling for the reality of God. This overpowering reality and concreteness of God took such possession of the Jewish people that it obliterated every other feeling, conception and purpose. In the meantime, the acceptance of the idea of immortality had become necessary for the further development of its historical destiny. The Jewish people was now faced with a new trial and experience. Doubt then made itself felt as to the equity of man's terrestrial destiny. It had already gained ground in the Hellenic and the ancient world in general with its instinctive faith in the immediate victory of goodness, truth and the just man. But the moment came when belief in this vanished and people began to feel that truth, goodness and the holy man did not receive their just award on earth. The holy man suffers and is crucified. This feeling is already apparent in the Book of Job, in the Proverbs of Solomon, in Orphism and in Plato. Later we have the attempts to discover another world and to situate the fulfilment of individual destiny on another plane. Thus the great religious problem of the Crucifixion and the just man, the bearer of the greatest good, has its origins both

[1]'The great pyramids are the most ancient and suggestive evidence available of the final rise of an organized society.' (Breastead.)

in the ancient Hebrew and Hellenic worlds. The death of Socrates had raised this problem in Greek culture, and it had served as the inspiration of Plato's philosophy. The death of Socrates compelled Plato to repudiate a world in which so just a man could be so undeservedly condemned, and it made him seek another world of goodness and beauty in which the unjust condemnation of the holy man was impossible. This motif recurs everywhere in the ancient world, the pagan as well as the Hebrew.

This extraordinary and acute spiritual experience was accompanied by an aspiration towards a different and higher world, where the solution of human destiny might be found. The growth of this kind of experience in the religious life of the pre-Christian world coincided with the transition from a national to an individual type of religious consciousness and with the development of religious individualism. The latter superseded the age of objectivism, which had mainly concerned itself with the life of the people or the nation in this terrestrial reality. The problem of the destiny demanding a solution outside the nation's vicissitudes now became the chief preoccupation. The period of objectivism was now supplanted by one of individualism. It was an age of transition. But this period of subjectivism prepared the ground for Christianity. The Christian truth was revealed to man at a time when the old national religious conceptions were beginning to disintegrate, and the human spirit began to be tormented by the problem of man's individual destiny which had failed to fulfil itself within the limits of either the Old Testament or paganism. This general transition from the objective-national to the subjective-individual conception coincided with the development of the doubts formulated by the Jewish messianic consciousness. The latter suffered an interior schism: it became divided, on the one hand, into a national messianic consciousness exclusively preoccupied with the terrestrial destiny and history of Israel; and, on the other, into a universal messianic consciousness living in the expectation of a Divine revelation. This universal revelation was to be a bearer of good tidings not only for Israel, but for the world in general and the individual soul of every man in particular.

Thus a process of interior division and disintegration was taking place in the old order of national religions. The human consciousness entered upon a path of individualism that was also the high road of universalism. The messianic idea was auspicious not only for mankind, as a whole, but for every individual human destiny. Such was the background of the whole tragedy. The ground was being made ready for Christianity. The Jewish people, animated by an intense feeling for history and aspiring towards the future, was destined to give birth to Christianity and bring about the central event of universal history, the revelation of the two worlds immanent and transcendental. The stage was now set for the greatest of all human tragedies in which the destiny of the Jewish people becomes linked up with that of the whole of Christian history. The rôle played by the Jews can be explained by their obsession with messianic expectations such as no other people entertained. Only they were haunted by that direct and immediate expectation of the coming of the Messiah. The other peoples of the pagan world had no more than a vague presentiment, no direct conscious communion with the future Messiah. But although the Jewish people was endowed with full messianic awareness and destined to give birth to the Messiah, it would not support the burden of its dualistic consciousness and expectation. As a result, it failed to comprehend the Coming of the Crucified. And here lies the essence of the tragedy that was to oppose Judaism and Christianity: the Messiah was destined to come among the Jewish people and the Jewish people could not accept a crucified Messiah. The Jewish people had longed for the Messiah and prophesied concerning Him; but it finally repudiated Him because it could not accept Him in the rôle of a servant. Its expectation had been of a king who would realize the kingdom of Israel on earth.

This intense longing symbolizes the religious collectivism of the Jewish people. It could accept neither Christ nor the mystery of His Crucifixion because he came as the bearer of a meek and not a triumphant truth on earth. His whole life and death were a repudiation of the longing for terrestrial beatitude cherished by the Jewish people. Thus Christianity restricts the divinity of the Jews to their consanguinity with Christ. They were a divine people in so far as Christ did come among them; but they ceased to be such after their repudiation of Him. After the Coming of Christ no Messianism in the old Hebrew sense of the word is possible. The later messianic expectations are therefore those of a false Messiah or Antichrist.

National Messianism, like class Messianism, always tends to fall back upon one or other forms of Judaism. Christendom's is the conjugation of the faithful. The result of the dualism inherent in Jewish Messianism has been to make every repudiation of Christ in the history of the world depend upon the same fundamental reasons and motives as had animated the false Messianism responsible for His Crucifixion. This carries with it the denial of spiritual freedom in the name of a compulsory fulfilment of the Kingdom of God upon earth. Christ was repudiated because He died on the Cross instead of using His kingly power to banish evil and suffering and institute the reign of justice and beatitude. This gives rise to a remarkable paradox, to that antithesis which Léon Bloy, that remarkable and insufficiently appreciated French writer, who died recently, formulated in his *Le Salut par les Juifs*. He sums up the fundamental tragedy of the Jewish people as follows: 'The Jews will be transformed only when Christ descends from the Cross, and Christ can descend from the Cross only when the Jews are transformed.' These penetrating words throw light not only upon the tragedy of the Jewish people, but also upon that of the Christian world; and they also disclose one of the fundamental objections raised against Christianity.

The main objection levelled against Christianity is that it has not fulfilled itself in the world, nor succeeded in imposing truth upon the earth and in banishing the sufferings which are still our mortal lot in the world. Some two thousand years ago Christ, the Saviour and Redeemer, came on earth; but evil, sufferings, horrors and torments still persist. This objection to Christianity is typical of that false Messianism founded upon the idea that the Coming of the Messiah, the Son of God, ought to bring with it the reign of goodness on earth. It demands a final victory over evil, the end of all suffering, torment and darkness, and the establishment of terrestrial beatitude. But the repudiation of the true Christ is an essentially Jewish one, although it is no less prevalent among the Aryans.

This brings us to the fundamental paradox of both Jewish and Christian history, namely, that the latter would have been impossible without the former. There would have been no Golgotha without the Jews, and yet they could not accept the mystery. But Christian history finds itself in inner conflict with the Jewish spirit. An inner trial was reserved for the former in its relation to the Jews. His connection with the Jews is a sore trial for the Christian spirit, and one which is far from being relieved either by the compliance and weakness of the Christians, which place them at the mercy of the Jewish spirit, or by racial anti-semitism which expresses itself in violence. Anti-semitism fails to grasp the religious gravity of the Jewish problem. Racial anti-semitism becomes infected with precisely that false Jewish spirit against which it is in revolt. Hatred of the Jews is a non-Christian feeling. Christians ought to treat the Jews in a Christian manner. Within Christian history itself there is a constant interaction of the Hebrew and Hellenic principles which together make up the main sources of our culture. The clash between these two principles extends, I believe, even into the domain of the Christian Church itself. Semitism has been grafted on to the Christian spirit and is indispensable to its destiny. Thus the theme of dualistic messianism, which first appears in Jewish history, has become that of universal history. The latter, in the centre of which stands Christ, develops round this theme. With the Coming of Christ a new universal era begins.

The Jewish problem is therefore insoluble within the limits of history. Sionism is powerless to solve it. The Biblical issue continues to rouse passions even in the nineteenth and twentieth centuries. The material shackles binding both the Capitalism of Rothschild and the Socialism of Marx to this world are Jewish in origin, although they are not now necessarily connected with the Jews. It is an idea that arouses the most bitter strife and passion. The Judaic hostility to Christianity is not confined to Jews, for Jews themselves may be exempt from it. The religious fulfilment of Jewish destiny cannot justify any vulgar Anti-semitism. An ultimate solution of the Jewish problem is possible only on the eschatological plane. Such a solution will coincide with that of universal history. And it will represent the last act in the struggle between Christ and Antichrist. Therefore the problem of universal history cannot be solved without the religious self-determination of Judaism.

CHAPTER VI

CHRISTIANITY AND HISTORY

In a preceding chapter I dealt at length with the extraordinary connection between Christianity and history. I quoted Schelling, who, in his *Verlesungen über die Methode des Academischen Studiums*, put forward the illuminating suggestion that Christianity was *par excellence* historical; that it represented, in fact, the revelation of God in history. I have also said that Christianity was by its nature a dynamic and impetuous force, as opposed to the contemplative and static religions of the ancient world. So great, indeed, is the dynamism of Christianity that it generates movement even in those spheres where its sway has been repudiated. This dynamism manifests itself in many different forms. One of these is the revolt against destiny which is peculiar to the Christian period of history, because Christianity is the source of both true and false principles of movement. The exclusively historical character and dynamism of Christianity are the result of the Coming of Christ, which constitutes the central fact of Christian history. This fact is unique and non-recurring,—the essential quality of everything historical. And it focuses the whole of world history.

The structure of the Christian world, which is based upon the unique and non-recurring character of the historical and the union of celestial and terrestrial history, is particularly complex; for it is based upon the play of all the fundamental forces previously active in history, and particularly upon the Judaic and Hellenic principles. Their conjunction and interaction, indeed, laid the foundations of Christian history. Their influence appears to dominate alternatively in one or other phase of Christian history.

The Judaic element stands for the principles of revealed law enunciated by the Old Testament. And, at certain moments, it exercises a determining influence upon the evolution of Christianity, emphasizing the Old Testament precepts of legality at the expense of the revelation of beatitude, love and freedom. It is, indeed, the source of pharisaism in the Christian world. But it may also be the source of a very different and apocalyptic spirit, aspiring towards new and ultimate revelations. The action of the latter, however, is opposed to the principles of the Old Testament. Nevertheless, both these Judaic principles, though by nature antithetical, are deeply historical in their contribution to tradition and aspiration towards the future.

It may be said that, on the whole, the Church is essentially and pre-eminently an historical force. It introduces revelation into the historical organization of mankind and guides the religious destinies of the national masses. It is thus an historical guiding force traditionally bound up with those Judaic principles which constitute the pre-eminently historical elements of Christianity. The Hellenic elements are also a rich source of Christianity, but they are less dynamic. They are mainly related to the contemplative side of Christianity. The whole of the Christian contemplative metaphysics, its dogma and mysticism, are Hellenic in origin; for the intense contemplation of the Divine Being is more peculiar to the Hellenic spirit than to the tempestuously moving, historical spirit of the Jews. All the aesthetics and beauty of Christianity derive from the former. It was, indeed, the source and cradle of beauty for the Christian world and the world in general for ages to come. The whole beauty of the Christian cult is based upon it. And the Protestant attempts to purge Christianity of its pagan elements have only contributed to weaken Christian aesthetics and metaphysics, that is, those elements pre-eminently associated with the Hellenic spirit.

The exceptionally dynamic and historical character of Christianity is the result of the fact that it conclusively revealed for the first time the existence of the principle of freedom, which was ignored by both the ancient and the Hebrew worlds. Christian freedom postulates the fulfilment of history through the agency of a free subject and spirit. And such a fulfilment constitutes the essential nature of both Christianity and history, because the structure of the latter is impossible without the postulate of a freely-acting subject determining the historical destinies of mankind. The Greeks affirmed the reason and necessity of good. To them it was the necessary result of the victory of reason. Socrates was the exponent of this Hellenic conception, which regarded good as based upon law and principles considered to be irrefutable by reason. The principles which contradict this were considered to be accidental and irrational. Thus the Greek conception of good took no account of freedom; and Greek philosophy, even at its height, never produced an authentic theory of good.

Christianity, on the other hand, affirmed the freedom of good. It affirmed that good is the product of the free spirit and that only such good can possess a true value and reality. It denied the compulsory and reasonable necessity of good. And this constitutes the essential feature of the Christian conception. Christianity affirmed that freedom is the highest achievement of the higher divine reason and that it determines the destiny of both man and the world, and thus makes history. Christian Providence is synonymous with freedom and not fatality. Unlike the ancient world, Christianity is not content to submit to fate. Such submissiveness as the highest wisdom attainable by man had been expressed in both Greek tragedy and philosophy. But the Christian spirit is based upon a principle that rebels against such submission. The freedom to choose and affirm the good, rooted in the will and not in reason, presupposes in its turn that freedom of the creative and active subject without which a true dynamism of history is impossible. The completely unhistorical or anti-historical nature of the ancient cultures of both India and China is due to the fact that the freedom of the creative subject was not revealed therein. Neither was it revealed in the philosophy of the Vedantas, one of the greatest philosophical systems, nor, again, in those philosophies which have a certain conception of freedom as an absolute blend and union of the human and divine spirits. India, too, ignored the idea of human freedom. And this accounts for the fact that this otherwise original culture lacks an historical character. Thus Christianity was the first to reveal conclusively the freedom of the creative subject which had been ignored by the pre-Christian world. And this discovery of the inner dynamic principles of history determining the fulfilment of the historical destinies of man, peoples and mankind, eventually produced that eventful world history which coincides with the Christian era.

What is the main theme of universal history? In my opinion it is that of man's destiny seen in the light of the interaction between the human spirit and nature, which constitutes the foundation and motivating principle of the 'historical'. We can observe in the history of mankind various stages of interaction between the human spirit and nature which fall into historical epochs. The initial stage, which was the direct result of the celestial-historical drama of man's alienation from God, of the Fall as a drama of freedom, had plunged man and the human spirit into the uttermost depths of natural necessity. The fall into these depths was accompanied by man's servitude to the natural elements which had held the human spirit and will spellbound. In the primal stages of history the human spirit is immersed in elemental nature; this is the state of the savage and barbarous peoples, the ancient cultures and the early history of the ancient world. The human spirit would seem to have lost its original freedom and have ceased to be even conscious of it. Immersed in the depths of necessity, man does not in his philosophy attain to the consciousness of freedom or of himself as a creative spiritual subject. The fact that the spellbound human spirit had lost its freedom as a result of its original alienation from the spirit of God explains why the true principle of freedom was not revealed in the ancient world. Freedom had been transformed into necessity, and the spirit was incapable of attaining either to a religious revelation or a philosophical apprehension of freedom.

The theme of man's worldly destiny is the liberation of the creative human spirit from the depths of natural necessity and its enslavement by the lowest elements. It was a theme that preoccupied the ancient world. The immersion of the human spirit in elemental nature is associated with man's bitter dependence on and torturing fear of the natural demons. The fallen human spirit, though rooted in and dominated by nature, was nevertheless in profound harmony with it. Man sensed natural life as a living organism, inspired and peopled with demons who were in perpetual contact with him; and its spiritual life was thus more familiar to him than in the subsequent stages of his history. Ancient myths speak of man's association with these natural spirits. The fallen human spirit had ceased to dominate nature and had of its own free will become the slave and indivisible part of nature in a prehistorical world. Man's dependence on nature was synonymous with his union with it. The pagan world was peopled with demons and man was powerless to dominate either them or the natural cycle. Man's image therefore corresponded not with the highest divine but the baser nature peopled with elemental spirits. Man adapted himself to the forms of this base nature, which had enslaved him and whose chains he could not break of his own free will.

The greatest contribution of Christianity, although it is not fully recognized by the Christian world, consisted in that it liberated man from the power of the baser elemental nature and demons. It did so through the agency of Christ and the mystery of Redemption. It rescued man forcibly from his immersion in elemental nature and revived his spirituality. It distinguished him from baser nature and set him up as an independent spiritual being, freeing him from submission to the natural world and exalting him to the heavens. Christianity alone restored the spiritual freedom of which man had been deprived by the power of the demons, the natural spirits and elemental forces in the pre-Christian world. The essential contribution of Christianity therefore lay in that it liberated man and offered a free solution for human destiny. And this is the high significance of man's Redemption from his outer and inner slavery, from those evil elements active in his own nature. His enslavement by the natural demons was, indeed, synonymous with his enslavement by his own baser self, from which he was unable to free himself because his freedom had become transformed into necessity. And this had come about through his own fault. But the Christian Redemption wrought by the coming of the Divine Man, the God-Man, the Man as the Second Hypostasis of the Divine Trinity, restituted the power of freedom and the image of his high divine origin to man, thus erasing the imprint of his slavery and animal origin. Only the coming of the Divine Man, His assumption of all the consequences of man's actions in the world, His sufferings and expiatory blood, and the mystery of the Redemption, could liberate man from the subjection of the baser elements and invest him once again with his lost Divine Sonship.

Ancient religions and mysteries had also aspired towards Redemption. The mysteries of Osiris, Adonis and Dionysos, were the obscure presentiments and passionate thirst for a true mystery of Redemption. In these mysteries man thirsted passionately to free himself from the slavery of nature and to achieve immortality; but the ancient mysteries never succeeded in achieving man's final liberation because they were involved in the cycle of baser elemental nature. They were immanent natural mysteries in which man experienced the joy of Redemption from his bitter state of subjection in the inmost depths of the natural cycle. Thus the mysteries of Dionysos were celebrated in the order of the natural cycles themselves, those of death and birth, winter and spring. But they failed either to exalt man above elemental nature or to achieve a real Redemption. The ancient world in celebrating these mysteries expressed a passionate thirst for deliverance; and, on the eve of its fall, it was more than ever gripped by the fear and terror of the natural demons. This terror reached its climax and became really unbearable in the last days of this world when the mystical cults extended their influence and power. The life of those who thirsted for Redemption became really tragic. Christianity alone saved man from this cycle of elemental natural life and re-established his dignity by restoring the freedom of the human spirit; and it thus inaugurated a new era in his destiny. The latter is now determined and solved by the agency of a free active subject, and man once again becomes conscious of his freedom.

There is a reverse side to this process of liberation which has sometimes been bitterly described as 'the death of the Great Pan'. For it is in this period of the collapse of the ancient world and birth of Christianity that a divorce takes place between man and the mysterious depths of natural life. The Great Pan, who had been revealed to the natural man of antiquity, was driven to take refuge in the uttermost depths of nature. A gulf now separated the natural man from the man who had entered upon the path of Redemption. The effect of Christianity was to divorce man from the inner life of nature, which, as a result, became de-animated. This was the reverse side of the Christian liberation of human nature. Thus in order to put an end of man's subservience to the natural spirits his access to them had to be prevented until he had attained spiritual maturity and achieved Redemption. For every new attempt of man to commune with paganism, which had culminated in the terror of the natural demons, would only threaten once again to bring about his fall. Christianity accomplished the process of liberating the human spirit by divorcing man from the inner life of nature. Nature remained part of that pagan world which it was necessary to renounce. And this was the position throughout the Middle Ages. The inner life of nature was a source of terror, and any communion with the natural spirits was looked upon as black magic. Christians feared nature because of its associations with paganism. Thus Christianity had effected man's deliverance from the terror and slavery of nature; but, in order to achieve this, it had been obliged to declare an uncompromising, passionate and heroic war on the natural elements both within and outside man, an ascetic war illustrated by the astounding lives of the Saints.

This repudiation of nature and loss of the keys to its inner life are the outstanding characteristics of the Christian as compared with the pre-Christian period of history. The consequences are at first sight paradoxical. The pagan world and all the ancient cultures had conceived nature as a living organism; but it had inspired the Christian world with dread and terror, and this led to its mechanization. There was the danger of communing with nature, the flight from and struggle against it. Later, at the dawn of modern history, technique begins to be applied to nature; and we have its complete mechanization as a result of its conception as a lifeless mechanism and not a living organism. This mechanization of nature is one of the secondary results of man's Christian liberation from demonolatry. In order to give back his freedom to man and discipline him, in order to distinguish him from nature and exalt him above it, Christianity had been obliged to mechanize nature.

However paradoxical it may seem, I am convinced that Christianity alone made possible both positive science and technique. As long as man had found himself in communion with nature and had based his life upon mythology, he could not raise himself above nature through an act of apprehension by means of the natural sciences or technique. It is impossible to build railways, invent the telegraph or telephone, while living in fear of the demons. Thus, for man to be able to treat nature like a mechanism, it is necessary for the daemonic inspiration of nature and man's communion with it to have died out in the human consciousness. The mechanical conception of the world was to lead to a revolt against Christianity, but it was itself the spiritual result of the Christian act of liberating man from elemental nature and its demons. When immersed in nature and communing with its inner life, man could neither apprehend it scientifically nor master it technically. This fact throws light on the whole of man's further destiny. Christianity had freed him from subjection to nature and had set him up spiritually in the centre of the created world. This anthropocentric feeling had been foreign to the man of classical antiquity, who had felt himself to be an inalienable part of nature. Christianity alone inspired man with this anthropocentric feeling which became the fundamental motivating power of modern times. It made modern history with all its contradictions possible, because it exalted man above nature. The recent adversaries of Christianity do not take sufficiently into account their own dependence upon this Christian principle.

The result of man's Christian liberation from nature was

that he retired into an inner spiritual world where he undertook a tremendous heroic struggle against the natural elements in order to overcome his subjection to baser nature, and to forge an image of himself as a free human personality. This great undertaking, one of the central facts of man's destiny, was achieved by the Christian Saints. The titanic struggle, conducted by the great Christian ascetics and hermits against the passions of the world, finally achieved man's liberation from the baser elements. In the ancient world the human image had been modelled upon that of the Old Adam, who, symbolizing collective mankind, had in prehistorical times fallen into the depths of baser elemental nature. But now man was obliged to renounce nature in order to forge a new human personality based upon that of the New Adam. This effort, which covers the periods of early coenobitism, mediaeval monasticism and all the ages in which this struggle for a new personality was waged, inaugurated the Christian era.

Christianity was the first to recognize the infinite value of the human soul, which it set above all the kingdoms of the world. For what use was it to win a world at the expense of one's soul? This idea is, indeed, one of the corner stones of the Evangelical doctrine. The struggle against the natural elements therefore became an essential part of Christianity. It gave rise to the Christian dualism of spirit and nature. This is not an ontological dualism. It is in the highest degree based upon a dynamic principle. The dynamism of history would be impossible without the opposition between the active subject and the objective natural environment against which he struggles. Accordingly, those periods of history in which the subject is entirely dominated by the environment do not favour historical dynamism.

Until the advent of Christianity the destiny of the whole of the ancient world was following a dual path, each aspect of which was to prove essential for the structure of universal history and the new era. The ancient world was tending towards universalism, that is, to transcend all particularism. The division of this world into the East and West, into a whole series of ancient cultures and peoples, into a multitude of particularist religions, was ultimately to be transcended by a process of unification which laid the foundations of a single great and universal spiritual and material whole. Alexander the Great's achievement in uniting the East and West helped tremendously this process of unification. The basis of spiritual unity was provided by the Hellenistic period which blended all the religions of the East and West. Its syncretic character permitted the assortment of all the cultural types peculiar to the ancient world. The formation of a single world state, the Roman Empire, was the direct result of the integrating process then going on, and laid the foundations of universal history, which dates from this period of the union of East and West. The historical rise and development of Christianity likewise took place in this period of pantheistic amalgamation, which witnessed the union of the Eastern and Western cultures and their final refraction in Roman culture. This process of unification, coinciding with the period of Hellenistic syncretism, made possible a spiritual unity of mankind which was far superior to the prophetic spirituality of the ancient Hebrews.

Particularism had been the feature of the ancient world. But the universality of Christianity had been predetermined by the unification of the East and West, first in Hellenistic culture and then in the Roman Empire. Christianity origin-

ated among an insignificant people who played no important part in the history of the time when the crucial events
were taking place in Rome or Alexandria. And yet Palestine,
though it was dominated by particularism and nationalism,
proved to be the scene of the greatest event in history, one
whose central significance became universally recognized.
For, indeed, the event that took place in Bethlehem determined the future history of the world. Great events were
taking place in the arena of history, in Rome, Egypt and
Greece; and the way was being paved for a universal union
of peoples and cultures. But the greatest, though a pin-point
in comparison with the others, was the revelation of the Divine presence. This great revelation and the confluent processes from above and below all united in one universal torrent in the last period of ancient history. The foundations of
the Christian world had been laid. This was one of the results
of the dual path followed by human destiny in the ancient
world.

The other very strange and tragic result was that the ancient world, although it had become unified, was about to
collapse. Its fall and that of paganism were imminent. The
great Hellenic culture and the great state of Rome were both
destined to suffer an eclipse. But this occurred only when the
foundations of a universal state had been laid. Thus, while the
high flowering of the ancient world dates back to the time of
comparatively small states without any claim to universal significance, might or glory, its disintegration coincides with
the attainment of both the universal idea and state, and also
with the spiritual refinements of later Hellenistic culture.

This, I believe, is one of the capital facts of world history,
and one which more than any other compels us to ponder on

the nature of the historical process and reconsider many of the theories of historical progress. The decline of the ancient world was no accident. It had been determined not only by the barbarian invasions which destroyed the treasures of the ancient world, but also by an inner disease, whose symptoms historians admit more and more readily, and which attacked its very roots and made its fall inevitable precisely in the period of its greatest superficial brilliance.

The fall of Rome and the ancient world teaches us two directly opposite things. It demonstrates the instability and fragility of all terrestrial things and cultural achievements; and it constantly reminds us that all cultural achievements are corruptible and contain the seed of their own decay when opposed to eternity. But in the light of history, this fall teaches us not only that culture has its stages of birth, flowering and decay, but that it is also based upon an eternal principle. For, while the ancient world was succeeded by a period of barbarism and darkness in the seventh, eighth and ninth centuries, it is also true to say that culture has survived the ages. It was deeply rooted in the life of the Christian Church, which combined the elements of Hellenic art and philosophy with the achievements of Roman culture. The fall of Rome and the ancient world then is not synonymous with death, but rather with a sort of historical catastrophe; an upheaval on the surface of the earth during which some new element is added to the foundations of history and the basic principle of ancient culture is left intact. Thus Roman law is still alive; and so are Greek art and philosophy and all the other ancient principles that constitute the foundations of our culture, which is one and eternal, though passing through various stages of existence. The collapse of the ancient world teaches us in the first place that all the doctrines of progress in a direct line will not bear serious examination. In fact, all the fundamental events of history constitute an essential denial of this theory.

Edward Meyer, one of the greatest historians of the ancient world, argues that cultures live through a period of development, flowering and decay. He believes that great cultures had existed in the ancient world compared with which many subsequent cultures would appear retrograde. The culture of Babylon, for example, was so perfect that in many respects it was in no wise inferior to that of the twentieth century. It is very essential for the philosophy of history to establish this point. Thus ancient Greece lived through a period of enlightenment which coincided with the development of Sophist criticism and is directly analogous to that of our eighteenth century. This enlightenment was supposed to triumph along a direct line of development. But history proves that the period of Greek enlightenment came to an abrupt end and was superseded by a great idealistic and mystical reaction, whose exponents were Socrates and Plato. This spiritual reaction against scepticism and rationalism was to run through the whole of the Middle Ages and thus stretches over a period of more than a thousand years. This fact is, however, absolutely incomprehensible from the standpoint of progressive enlightenment. How are we to account for such a lasting reaction? Many modern historians of Greece, such as Beloc, for example, are hostile to this spiritual current, and see in Plato the initiator of a reaction which lasted until the time of the Renaissance. But why then did the 'enlightenment' not continue? This brings us to a very interesting problem of the philosophy of history.

Christianity had its rise in the Hellenistic period, that late flower and refinement of ancient culture, and it therefore contains no traces of the naïveté peculiar to primitive religions. This fact is very important in explaining the character of Christianity. It is not a natural religion directly associated with a feeling for nature and the reproduction of its mysterious organic processes in the soul. It is, rather, a cultural-historical religion which reveals the mystery of life and the Divine Being by means of the dualism of the soul that has already discarded its naïve feeling for and associations with nature. This aspect is essential to any definition of Christianity, which forms the point of intersection for the two great directions of universal history; and which once again raised and solved the great problem of East and West. Christianity was the meeting ground of the Eastern and Western spiritual and historical forces. It is, in fact, inconceivable without this union. And yet it is the only universal religion which, though having its immediate origin in the East, stands out as being *par excellence* the religion of the West, whose peculiarities it reflects. The final union of the East and West had, of course, been prepared by Hellenistic culture and the material conquests of Rome; and that had laid the foundations of a united mankind. Christianity, therefore, supplied the postulate of universal history without which a philosophy of history is altogether impossible. Thus, while establishing itself upon the ground of a united East and West, Christianity offered the postulate of a united mankind and a Providence manifesting itself in historical destinies. But Christianity at the same time transferred the centre of gravity from East to West. World history followed in the wake of this new sun. And the peoples of the East, who had contributed the first pages to the history of mankind and had given birth to the first great cultures and religions, now seem to vanish from world history. The East becomes increasingly static. The dynamic force of history was transferred wholly to the West. Christianity had introduced historical dynamism into the life of the Western peoples. The East fell back upon inner contemplation and retired from the arena of world history. Thus, in so far as the East remained non-Christian, it failed to participate in world history. This is a practical proof that Christianity was the greatest dynamic force and that those peoples, who finally failed to accept and follow it, ceased to be dynamic peoples.

I do not mean to imply that the East is moribund or that it contains no further possibilities of life. On the contrary, I am inclined to think that the Eastern peoples will once again join the torrent of history and that they will once again play a rôle of world importance. The World War, from whose consequences we are still suffering, will have helped to draw them again into the vortex of universal history. It may, perhaps, bring about another universal union of East and West transcending the limits of European culture; and we may again live through something analogous to the Hellenistic epoch. But of the past we can only say that, at a given moment, the East ceased to be the motivating force of history. I do not include Russia in the East. I consider Russia to be an original blend of East and West. This fact helps to explain the complexity of her historical destiny, which differs from that of the non-Christian peoples of the East.

All I have said concerning the liberation of the human spirit from the depths of nature, the human personality and man as the image and counterpart of God, was by way of emphasizing the fact that Christianity was the first to become conscious of the human personality and raise the problem of its eternal destiny. A really profound investigation of this problem had been impossible in the ancient pagan and Hebrew worlds. But Christianity had affirmed the spiritual primacy and priority of human nature, and it had denied its origin in any lower nature or non-human environment. It associated the human personality directly with the highest divine nature and origin; and that explains its deep antagonism to the evolutionary-naturalistic conception of man. For whereas the latter studies man as a child of the world and nature, and denies his spiritual or high aristocratic origin, Christianity affirms man's primordial nature, independence and, above all, his freedom from the baser elemental processes. This made possible the apprehension for the first time of both the human personality and its high inherent dignity. Thus the development of the human personality constitutes the peculiar achievement of the Christian period of history.

The human personality was, indeed, forged and fortified in the Middle Ages—that period which the humanists had long considered to be unfavourable to its development. Monasticism and Chivalry were the two forces which contributed most to strengthen and discipline man's spiritual life in the Middle Ages. The models of the monk and knight were precisely those of a disciplined personality, which was thus protected by both a spiritual and physical armour against the elemental and disrupting forces of the external world. Too little attention has been paid to the tremendous influence exercised by the Middle Ages on the formation of the European man who, in a burst of extraordinary energy, reached his full stature and asserted his rights in the age of the

Renaissance. And this result was attained chiefly through the concentration of man's spiritual forces and the forging of the human personality on the model of the monk and knight, which helped to strengthen the principle of human liberty. Indeed, the whole significance of Christian asceticism lay in this concentration of spiritual forces and the refusal to waste them. Man's creative forces were concentrated and preserved when not allowed to express themselves with sufficient freedom. This proved to be one of the greatest and most unexpected contributions of mediaeval history; and the long period of creative economy made possible the creative outburst of the Renaissance. Thus European man would not have crossed the threshold of modern history full of creative power and daring had he not passed through the ascetic school of restraint. This explains, too, the essential difference between mediaeval and modern history. For European man to-day is emerging from modern history exhausted and with all his creative forces spent. He had, on the other hand, emerged from the Middle Ages with accumulated and virgin forces, disciplined in the school of asceticism. The model of the monk and knight had preceded the Renaissance and, without them, the human personality would never have been able to exalt itself to its destined heights.

But the decline of the Middle Ages, which was to inaugurate modern history and the epochs of the Renaissance and humanism, also denoted that they could not solve their essential problems. It demonstrated that the mediaeval idea of the Kingdom of God had not been fulfilled, and that this failure had incited man to rebel in the age of the Renaissance. The great contribution of the Middle Ages lies not only in that it unfolded its ideal, but also in that it disclosed the contradictions inherent in it and its ultimate impracticability. The Middle Ages were bound to break down on this issue. Theocracy was neither achieved nor could it very well impose itself by force of arms. The ultimate achievement of the Middle Ages lay rather in the concentration of man's spiritual forces for the creation of a new world than in the realization of their particular aims. The results of a historical movement are usually quite different from the ideals which consciously inspire it. Thus the ultimate result of the process which led to the foundation of the Roman Empire was not the fact of its foundation; for its duration was limited and culminated in its disintegration and fall. But that disintegration laid the foundations of a united mankind which in its turn proved to be the basis for the Catholic Christian Church.

In the same way, I believe that the Middle Ages unconsciously forged the human personality which was to manifest itself in modern history. The mediaeval consciousness had been chiefly preoccupied with the ideals of theocracy and feudalism or new forms of Chivalry, but all these either proved to be failures or were swept away by modern history. A distinction must, however, be made between these external forms and the spiritual principles which are eternal. But already a Christian Renaissance was taking place in the thirteenth and fourteenth centuries within the framework of the Middle Ages. It was characterized by the revival of ancient classical forms; and Scholasticism itself symbolized the victory of a classical form in philosophy. But its highest expression was reached in Dante.

CHAPTER VII

THE RENAISSANCE AND HUMANISM

In the Middle Ages man's energies were concentrated upon interior spiritual matters and were not sufficiently manifested in exterior forms. Yet the Middle Ages culminated in the Christian Renaissance which represents the highest point reached in the development of Western European culture. I am thinking of the mystical Renaissance of Italy, which comprehends the prophecies of Joachim of Floris, the saintliness of Saint Francis of Assisi and the genius of Dante. I likewise associate with it the paintings of Giotto and all the currents of earlier Italian art. Taken as a whole this is one of the most extraordinary moments in the spiritual culture of Western Europe. It also raised the problem of a purely Christian Renaissance, and laid the foundations of a purely Christian humanism which must be distinguished from the later humanism of modern history.

This Christian humanism stands out above all other contributions of Western spiritual culture. The purpose behind the mediaeval religious culture was by its depth and universal aim perhaps the greatest in history. It was such also by the scope of its imagination and ideal, which aspired to establish the Kingdom of God on earth surpassing in beauty all that had ever been conceived, and which evidenced a partial return to Greek sources, since every regeneration implies a revival of the latter. But this grandiose design of religious culture was doomed to failure; and the mediaeval Kingdom of God was neither fulfilled nor could be fulfilled. The achievements of the Christian Renaissance were, however, as extraordinary as the saintliness of Saint Francis and the genius of Dante; but this creative spiritual experience only served to demonstrate that man could no longer pursue the path which had been laid down for him by the mediaeval consciousness. His further path led him away from mediaeval culture. It led him in another direction, towards another Renaissance, which was in many ways anti-Christian.

The later Renaissance contained the elements of both the early Christian and the anti-Christian humanism. This constitutes the theme of man's destiny, which is at the same time the fundamental theme of the philosophy of history. The Renaissance is therefore one of the decisive moments in man's destiny. The mediaeval consciousness had certain defects and insufficiencies which were to become increasingly apparent towards the end of the Middle Ages and the beginning of modern times. Wherein, then, lay the defect of this mediaeval idea of the Kingdom of God? For in virtue of it the mediaeval world came to an end and its theocratic culture was faced with an internal crisis and disaster; the mediaeval gave place to the modern world, which was animated by a spirit hostile to the former. I believe that the defects of the mediaeval consciousness lay in that it did not allow for the free play of man's creative energies. In the mediaeval world man had not the power to create or to build up a culture freely; and thus man's spiritual forces, which had been forged by Christianity in the mediaeval period, had not been given a free trial in this sphere. Mediaeval asceticism had strengthened man's spiritual forces, but had prevented their free participation in the work of creative culture. It became clear that a compulsory fulfilment of the Kingdom of God was impossible. The latter could not be established without the free consent and participation of man's autonomous forces. The revelation of man's forces and creative energies was necessary to religious culture in the world. It was necessary that man should pass freely through this trying and tragic experience; that he should at last discover higher forms of religious consciousness; and that he should be able to establish autonomously a theonomic culture and devote his creative energies to the fulfilment of the Kingdom of God.

Modern history constitutes an attempt to discover man's potentialities. And in order to give them full play, humanism evolves a new type of European man. The Middle Ages had concentrated and disciplined man's spiritual forces, but they had at the same time curbed them. They held man in subjection to a spiritual authority and thus centralized all human culture. This subordination was in the very order of mediaeval culture. But, at the dawn of modern times, a decentralization took place and man's creative forces were suddenly liberated. Their ebullience produced that spiritual revolution which we call the Renaissance, the consequences of which were still making themselves felt in the nineteenth century. It brought with it the liberation of man's creative forces, spiritual decentralization and the differentiation of all the spheres of social and cultural life. Science, art, political and economic life, society and culture now become autonomous. This process of differentiation is synonymous with the secularization of human culture. Even religion is secularized. Art and science, the state and society, enter the modern world along a

[130]

secular path. The bonds holding together the various spheres of social and cultural life now become relaxed, and these spheres become independent. That is the essential character of modern history. The transition from mediaeval to modern history is synonymous with one from the divine to the human aspects of the world, from the divine depths, interior concentration and the inner core, to an exterior cultural manifestation. This divorce from the spiritual depths, in which man's forces had been stored and to which they had been inwardly bound, is accompanied not only by their liberation, but by their passage from the depths to the periphery and the surface of human life, from the mediaeval religious to secular culture; and it implies the transference of the centre of gravity from the divine depths to purely human creation. The spiritual bond with the centre of life grows gradually weaker. Modern history therefore conducts European man along a path which removes him ever further from the spiritual centre. It is the path of man's free experience and the trial of his creative forces.

Burckhardt says that the Renaissance discovered man and the individual. But what does the discovery of man signify? It is more correct to say that man's inner being was discovered in the Middle Ages, when he was engaged in spiritual work and stood in the centre of Christian faith and Creation, although the attitude to man then was quite different from that current in the age of the Renaissance. The Renaissance once more discovered the natural man, the old Adam of the pre-Christian world, for whom Christianity had substituted the new Adam or the spiritual man. Christianity had declared war on the natural man and on the baser elements in the name of a spiritual forging of the human per-

[131]

sonality and for the sake of man's Redemption. Mediaeval Christianity had bound the natural man hand and foot; it was engaged in forging human forces, and it divorced man from both the nature within him and that of the environing world. In the Middle Ages nature was a closed book. Communion with it had been one of the fundamental aspects of the ancient life whose associations with it had been deeply rooted. The modern man's discovery of nature therefore implied that of antiquity. The Renaissance represented the discovery of both nature and antiquity. This communion with the natural foundations of human life and the discovery of creative forces in the natural sphere prepared the ground for humanism. The humanist consciousness, which was the result of the double communion with nature and antiquity, diverted its contemplation from the image of the spiritual man to that of the natural man. It released man's natural forces and at the same time severed his connection with the spiritual authority, divorcing the natural from the spiritual man. The discovery of his natural forces and of a new consciousness upon their basis inspired man with a youthful confidence in himself and his creative possibilities. Man's forces appeared to be boundless, and there seemed to exist no limits to human creation in either art or science, political or social life. On the threshold of modern history man would seem to have a wonderful future ahead of him. He feels the liberation of his force and a profound and direct communion with natural life and antiquity.

It is a curious fact that in Italy, which saw the flowering of man's creative forces, no revolt against Christianity took place. Italy had always preserved her associations with antiquity through Rome; the connection had never been lost and the ideas of antiquity had never become altogether alien to Italian history. The Italian Renaissance, therefore, far from breaking with the Catholic Church, preserved a curious association with the Catholic faith, an association at times under Papal patronage. The Renaissance manifested itself with extraordinary force in the Vatican. The result was to enrich Catholicism itself. This fact distinguishes the temperament of the Romance from that of the Nordic or Germanic peoples which ultimately gave rise to the Protestant revolt. But the Italian and Romance temperaments in general, aesthetically attached to the cult of the Church, did not attempt any such revolutionary act. They encouraged positive creation rather than a revolt against the religious and spiritual past.

What was the essence of man's communion with nature and antiquity? It was the search after perfect forms in all spheres of human creation. A formal principle of this sort in human creation always denotes a Renaissance approach to antiquity. I have often repeated that the essential feature of the whole order of Hellenic culture lies in the mastery of a form which reaches an immanent perfection. Every attempt to formalize thought, artistic creation, politics and law, represents a return to antiquity. I believe that Patristic thought, in so far as it involved a return to Plato and Aristotle, represents an attempt to give form to the Christian content by means of Hellenic ideas. But the return to ancient forms was immeasurably more striking at the dawn of modern times.

The search after new perfect forms has two aspects. On the one hand, it implies a direct communion with the ancient art, philosophy and state. On the other, the search for perfect forms is carried into nature itself. The Renaissance turns man's attention to nature in such a way as to direct his creative researches towards the discovery of perfect forms in and through nature itself. The search after the source of perfection in the perfect forms of nature itself predetermines the currents of art. The art of the Renaissance studies the perfection of forms in nature as well as in ancient art. And this constitutes its profound essence. It symbolizes the search after perfect forms on the part of the new spirit which, emerging from mediaeval history, turns for inspiration to ancient art, science, politics and all forms of ancient life, although it had no real affinity with the spirit of the ancient world. The Renaissance marks the turbulent and passionate clash of the new spiritual content of Christian life which had slowly formed itself in the course of the Middle Ages; of the human soul which had developed a nostalgia for another transcendental world and was unable to find satisfaction in this world; with the eternally renascent and regenerating antique forms. It was a soul stricken with thirst for Redemption and for communion with its mystery which was ignored by the ancient world; a soul poisoned by the Christian consciousness of sin and the Christian division between two worlds; a soul incapable of being satisfied by either the forms of natural life or the culture of the ancient world.

The Renaissance is deeply marked by that dualism of consciousness which it inherited from the experience of the Middle Ages with their antitheses between God and devil, heaven and earth, body and soul. It thus united the Christian transcendental consciousness, which breaks through all barriers with the immanent consciousness of ancient naturalism. The Renaissance did not at any moment constitute an integral unity of its own. It could not be an absolute revival of paganism. It was an unusually complex phenomenon, for it was founded upon the turbulent clash of the pagan and the Christian, of the eternally immanent and the transcendental principles of human nature. This refutes the theory that the Renaissance was the revival of paganism, that it gave birth to a pagan joy of life which aspired towards nature, that the Renaissance man finally broke away from Christian principles and that the epoch was dominated by one very well defined and distinct tone. Historians now admit that the Renaissance represents the tempestuous clash of two principles, and that both the pagan and the Christian principles were active in it. This fact stands out particularly clearly in that notable record of the epoch, Benvenuto Cellini's autobiography. Benvenuto Cellini may be regarded as a sixteenth century pagan: he commits the most dastardly crimes and sets his stamp upon the age in which such crimes were common enough. And yet he remains a Christian; he has mystical visions in the castle of Sant' Angelo. If this is true of Benvenuto Cellini, who lived in the later period of the Renaissance and who was further removed from the mediaeval Christian principles, it must be still more true of the earlier stages. The men of the quattrocento all bear the mark of this dualism. And the Renaissance finally proves the impracticability of a classical perfection of form and clarity in a Christian period of history. The Christian spirit which had discovered heaven and transcended the limits of the world, which could conceive life as closed and immanent, found it impossible to achieve those perfect forms which the classical world had succeeded in creating when it produced the image of a terrestrial Eden and of the perfect beauty of terrestrial life. It had been possible to do so only once in universal history. Christian history, however, gives examples of periodical attempts at a revival of or a return to the Hellenic world whose beauty captivates the soul. But the Christian world found it impossible to equal this beauty, this clarity and integrity of the spirit. This is mainly due to the cleavage introduced by the Christian consciousness between heaven and earth, between eternal and temporal life, between the transcendentally infinite and the immanently hermetic worlds,—a cleavage that is insurmountable within the limits of terrestrial history and culture.

Christianity establishes a type of culture and creation in which all achievements are symbolic. Thus the art of the Christian world is by its nature symbolic and not classical. But symbolic achievements tend to be always imperfect and lacking in clarity, because they presuppose a form denoting the existence of an Absolute beyond the limits of a given terrestrial achievement. The symbol is a bridge between two worlds: it affirms that the perfect form is attainable only beyond a certain boundary, but not in the closed circle of terrestrial life. This inability to arrive at a perfection of form is particularly evident in the quattrocento or the middle period of the Renaissance. This period of great research is characterized by its imperfection of form. The imperfection of the terrestrial form implies a super-terrestrial perfection. The art of the time does not so much create perfection as confess its nostalgia for it and express it symbolically. This is the characteristic feature of the whole order of Christian culture. It will become particularly clear if we compare Classical and Gothic architecture. While the former achieves a final perfection as in the dome of the Pantheon, the latter is essentially imperfect. Nor does it strive after perfection of form. It aspires to the heavens quivering with anguish and nostalgia, and proclaims that the achievement of perfection is possible only there; on earth only anguish and a passionate longing for it are possible.

This impossibility of terrestrial perfection constitutes the peculiarity of the Christian culture. By its very nature the latter could not ultimately fulfil itself. It symbolizes the principle of an eternal search, longing and aspiration; and it is but the symbolic reflection of the possibilities beyond the limits of this earth. The antagonism of the Christian and pagan souls attains its acutest and most beautiful expression in the work of Botticelli, the greatest painter of the quattrocento. In his art the dualism of the Renaissance man, the clash of the pagan and Christian principle, reaches a particular intensity of expression. Botticelli's creative path led him in the end to follow in the footsteps of Savonarola,—a tragedy comparable only to that of Gogol when he burned his manuscripts. The work of Botticelli reflects, too, the inability of the Christian soul to attain to perfection in artistic forms, its sickness and disintegration, and its failure to fulfil itself in cultural creation. It was said of Botticelli that his Venuses had abandoned the earth and that his Madonnas had abandoned him. The inability to arrive at a perfect image of the Madonna in this terrestrial existence constitutes the characteristic trait of Botticelli's spirit; and in this lies his whole nostalgia.

I find Botticelli's art both beautiful and illuminating because the Renaissance was destined to suffer an inner failure. The essence and greatness of the latter consists, perhaps, in that it neither did nor could succeed; a purely pagan Renaissance concerned exclusively with terrestrial forms was impossible in a Christian world. A profound disillusionment with the possibility of realizing perfect forms on earth was as inevitable to this world as the search after them or the communion with ancient forms. Thus it becomes impossible to achieve an immanent perfection in the Christian period of history. And the failure of the Rensissance constitutes, perhaps, its greatest achievement, because it makes possible the realization of the maximum of creative beauty. The dualistic vision of the quattrocento contributes a profound knowledge of man's destiny and provides a striking demonstration of the limits of man's creative expression in the Christian period of universal history. The Coming of Christ and the Redemption had invalidated the intrinsic perfection of creative forms.

It might be objected that the cinquecento attained to a much greater perfection of forms. The art of Michael Angelo and Raphael would seem to have achieved a real perfection. But an amazing destiny awaited sixteenth century Italian art at the height of its perfection. For Raphael's art, that high peak of attainment, coincided with the beginning of the decadence of the Renaissance. An interior lack of soul becomes apparent in Raphael's masterpieces which otherwise succeeded in achieving perfection of composition. But we miss in them that interior pulsation which makes itself felt in quattrocento art. And, moreover, the Bolognese and Baroque schools, which succeeded those of the cinquecento, were already manifestly decadent.

A return to the creative epochs of the past implies not only a simple imitation of them, but also the revival usually of ancient and eternal principles which appear refracted in the new ones. Thus the age of the Renaissance marked not only the return to and imitation of ancient forms, but also an original adaptation of them to the new spirit and the new content, and thus produced entirely new results. The affinity, too, between the ancient and the Renaissance worlds has been much exaggerated. Renaissance art fails to reproduce antique perfection; and this is natural enough since nothing ever recurs. Renaissance Platonism bears but a slight resemblance to that of the ancient world. The same is true of the attempts to set up artificial political forms on the model of the antiquity which they do not at all resemble. Such resemblances as exist are merely superficial and illusory. In reality the whole creative culture of the Renaissance is much less perfect than the Hellenic at its flowering-time. The latter has perhaps never been surpassed in human history. Nevertheless, the Renaissance is both richer and more fruitful in its researches, as well as much more complex than the simpler but more integral culture of Greece.

The inner guiding spirit of modern history, which had inspired the Renaissance in the fifteenth and sixteenth centuries and continued to do so throughout modern history, is only now beginning to abandon its sway. This was the humanist spirit which lies at the foundations of all modern conceptions. The beginning of the humanist era coincided with that of modern times. The Renaissance was soon a fact not only in Italy, but throughout Europe. Shakespeare's work was one of its greatest manifestations. It revealed that free play of creative energies which followed man's liberation from his mediaeval confinement. The Renaissance spirit manifests itself in all European countries, but it reached its flower of perfection in Italy. Humanism constitutes indeed the leaven of modern history. To understand its spirit is to grasp the very essence of the latter. It is to comprehend the whole of man's destiny in it and the inevitability of his experience down to our day. It is to define and explain these experiences. I personally believe that humanism was founded upon a deep contradiction whose expression forms the very theme of modern history. This essential contradiction explains all the disillusions of modern history and human destiny; those disillusions which have assailed human freedom and poisoned the joy of human creation. It explains all the bitter disappointments experienced by us down to our own times. But wherein does this contradiction lie?

Humanism, as its name implies, denotes the elevation and setting up of man in the centre of the universe. It signifies his rebellion, affirmation and discovery. This is one of its aspects. It has been said that humanism discovered the human individuality and gave it full play, freeing it from its mediaeval subjection and directing it upon free paths of self-affirmation and creation. But humanism also contained a diametrically opposed principle, that of man's abasement, of the exhaustion of his creative powers and of his general enfeeblement. For humanism, by regarding man as part of nature, transferred the centre of gravity of the human personality from the centre to the periphery. It divorced the natural from the spiritual man. It divorced him from the interior significance and the divine centre of life, from the deepest foundations of man's very nature; and it then gave him the freedom of creative development. In fact, humanism denied that man was the image and likeness of God; that he was the reflection of the Divine Being[1]. In its dominant form humanism affirmed that human nature was the image and likeness not of the di-

[1]An exception must be made in favour of the early Christian humanism; and in that of Paracelsus, Pico della Mirandola, Erasmus and Saint Thomas More.

vine but of universal nature. It affirmed that man was a natural being, the child of the world and of nature, created by natural necessity, the flesh and blood of the natural world; and that he therefore shared all its limitations, diseases and defects. Thus humanism not only affirmed man's self-confidence and exalted him, but it also debased him by ceasing to regard him as a being of a higher and divine origin. It affirmed exclusively his terrestrial birth place and origin at the expense of the celestial. In this way humanism helped to diminish man's stature. The result of man's self-affirmation, once he had ceased to be conscious of his tie with the higher Divine and Absolute nature and with the highest source of his life, was to bring about his own perdition. Humanism dethroned the Christian spiritual principle, which had considered man in the image and likeness of God, of the child of God and as a being deriving Sonship from God. The Christian consciousness of man began to lose its strength. And this, in its turn, gave rise to a self-destructive dialectic within humanism.

Humanism passed through various stages. The nearer it kept to the Christian and Catholic sources, and thus to the ancient ones, the finer and more powerful was its creative effort. But the further it departed from the Middle Ages and the more it denied its ancient foundations, the sooner did its creative powers become exhausted and the beauty of the human spirit enfeebled. This is one of the most indubitable as well as paradoxical situations disclosed by modern history. It explains the terrible lack of correspondence between the beginnings and the end of humanism, between its flowering-time in the age of the Renaissance, when the mediaeval and Catholic foundations of the human personality as well as their tie with antiquity still made themselves felt, and its culminating phase, when an ever greater rupture with the mediaeval Catholic foundations, and therefore with antiquity, became apparent. For the further man's consciousness and history led him away from the mediaeval principles, the further he departed from those of antiquity, thus betraying the original covenant of the Renaissance.

The essential principles of antiquity had never really died out, particularly among the Romance peoples. The new spirit which manifested itself in modern history opened up absolutely new vistas for man which had nothing in common with those of either his ancient or mediaeval destiny. And yet man's spiritual foundations are two,—the Hellenic and the mediaeval Christian or Catholic. This seemingly paradoxical assertion brilliantly confirms the whole dialectic of man. The latter is contained in the fact that *man's self-affirmation leads to his perdition; the free play of human forces unconnected with any higher aim brings about the exhaustion of man's creative powers.* The passionate striving to create beauty and perfect forms, which inaugurated the Renaissance period of history, culminates only in their destruction and enfeeblement. This becomes apparent in every sphere of human culture.

The Renaissance period of history submits human freedom to a great trial. But this latter was providentially inevitable. The establishment of the Kingdom of God would be impossible without such a free trial of human forces. The latter had not formed part of the mediaeval project of a theocracy on earth. But mankind could not achieve the Kingdom of God without the freedom of creation. It is one thing to affirm the inevitability of this process of modern history and to recognize the profound significance of man's humanist experience, and another to affirm that humanism is based upon the highest authentic truth and that it represents the highest attainment of human forces and freedom. I believe that man has lived through schism and decadence, and their consequences; but he has had to do so in the name of the greatest purpose underlying every free experience. This contradiction manifest in humanism constitutes the theme of the philosophy of modern history. Its discovery brings us to the end of the Renaissance and of humanism which we are experiencing in its acutest form. This also brings us to the end of modern history. And we are now entering upon an absolutely unknown period, the fourth period of universal history, which has as yet no name. It denotes, too, the final bankruptcy of both the Renaissance and humanism.

The Reformation was the next stage in the development of humanism in modern history. It followed the unexampled manifestation of man's creative forces during the Renaissance, and it was accompanied by a dialectic of its own. The mission had now passed to another race. The Renaissance had its origins in the south, among the Romance peoples: the Reformation was the contribution of the northern and pre-eminently Germanic peoples. It was the creation of another racial temperament, the expression of another spirit. It reflected the positive as well as negative qualities of the German race. The German Reformation exhibited certain traits of the German spirit which set it in some respects above the Romance spirit. These were a particular profundity and striving after spiritual purity. The result of this was to endow both the Renaissance and humanism with a religious form. The Romance Catholic world had been the scene of a creative humanist revival which did not take the form of a revolt against the Catholic Church. The Popes had patronized the

Renaissance and had themselves been inspired by the Renaissance spirit. But decadence had set in within the Church, particularly in the governmental spheres; and it was against this that the German race revolted. Its revolt assumed the character of a protest rather than of a creative manifestation. The humanism of the German Reformation affirms both the true freedom of human nature as against the compulsion which had been exercised in the Catholic world and the false freedom which was to lead man to his perdition. Such was the essential contribution of the Reformation: on the one hand,—and this was its most authentic and positive act, —it affirmed man's freedom; and on the other, it placed him on a lower plane than the Catholic consciousness had done.

This latter thought requires development. The Catholic Christian consciousness had affirmed the existence of two principles, the divine and the human. It had also affirmed man's independence before God and recognized both the inter-relation of these two principles and their independent origin. The Protestant Lutheran consciousness, on the other hand, affirmed the existence uniquely of God and the Divine Nature, denying the independence of human nature. This is a monism, but one that is opposed to a naturalistic monism. The religious and mystical consciousness of Protestantism therefore affirmed uniquely God and the Divine Nature, and denied man's original independence and the ontological foundations of human liberty. Luther affirmed the freedom of the religious consciousness. In his protest against Catholicism he asserted the autonomy of man's religious consciousness, but he denied the primal foundations of man's freedom. He tended to subscribe to the Augustinian doctrine of Grace which left no room for man's freedom. This tendency is characteristic not only of the Reformation, but also of the whole of the spirit behind German philosophy and idealist monism. The unique divine principle is revealed within man, but the latter's independent nature and freedom before the divine principle is denied. Thus abstract German mysticism and idealism tend to regard human nature as a secondary nature in no way related to the essence of being. This doctrine was already implicit in the Reformation, which had begun to deny metaphysically the human freedom it had first of all affirmed. Thus the Reformation contains an anti-humanist as well as a humanist principle. Moreover, it wished to exterminate the pagan principle in Christianity and was hostile to all its Hellenic sources. It laid the foundations of a spiritual current which departed ever further from the ideal of classical beauty and antique forms. It is therefore an essential stage in the development of the humanist dialectic. But, before approaching the fundamental theme of the decline of the Renaissance, it is important to consider the principal stages of this dialectic.

The age of eighteenth-century enlightenment, which was closely connected with the coming of the new man in the epoch of the Renaissance, forms the next stage. The disintegration of humanism is already apparent. The spirit of 'enlightenment' does not at all resemble that of the flowering-time of the Renaissance. Its rationalism lacks that full enthusiasm and faith in the power and possibilities of man's knowledge which was the feature of the Renaissance with its belief that man was able to master the mysteries of nature. Both the theosophic and the natural-philosophic currents of the Renaissance gave proof of the extraordinary progress which had been made in the study of the mysteries of nature. They conceived the latter as being something divine and living, something with which man had to commune and blend. The first great discoveries of natural science contributed still further to this progress. But the age of enlightenment in spite of all its faith in reason lacks this enthusiasm for the knowledge of nature. Reason itself begins to be undermined: its quality is affected because the tie with the higher reason uniting man with the divine cosmos has become weakened. This, of course, marks the beginning of that isolation and divorce of man from the spiritual principles which ultimately leads to his divorce from cosmic life. The consequences of this process become already apparent in the nineteenth century. Like the Renaissance, the Reformation, and the age of enlightenment which had preceded it, the French Revolution was but another great manifestation of the humanist spirit in modern history. It marks one of the essential stages in the destiny of both the Renaissance and the humanist self-affirmation. The latter was destined to lead inevitably to the acts of the French Revolution and to the trial of man's forces in this domain. Those elements which had been confined to the sphere of art and science in the Renaissance, to that of religion in the Reformation, and to that of reason in the age of enlightenment, were now applied in the sphere of communal and collective action. Thus man's faith in his ability as a natural being to change absolutely freely and independently human society and the direction of history; his belief in his perfect freedom from control and in his right to proclaim and fulfil this freedom; all these now manifest themselves in communal and collective action. In this sphere, then, the French Revolution realized one of the greatest of humanist experiments. It was an experiment which served to verify the interior contradictions, problems and consequences of a humanism divorced from its spiritual foundations. But the French Revolution was powerless to solve its own problems: it could realize neither man's rights nor the freedom of human life. It suffered a defeat. It succeeded only in realizing tyranny and abusing man. The Renaissance had been a great manifestation of man's creative powers, but it had failed to achieve the perfection of terrestrial forms. The Reformation had put forward the temptation of freedom only to reveal its religious impotence and to assume negative and not creative forms. And now the Revolution was attended with a still greater failure.

The French Revolution had proved a failure, as witness the whole of the nineteenth century. And the spiritual reaction, which set in at the beginning of that century and which is still developing in our day, lays bare the essence and meaning of this failure. It became clear that the Revolution could not help man to realize his rights, freedom or happiness. For the Revolution which, in 1789, had been animated by the ideal of the Rights of Man, of the citizen and of freedom, arrives by 1793 at the negation of all rights and of all freedom. It consumes itself, thus revealing that it possessed at the foundations no ontological principle to justify the rights of man. It becomes apparent then that the rights of the man, who forgets those of God, tend to exterminate themselves without liberating him. The spiritual reaction at the beginning of the nineteenth century clearly demonstrated this. It contributed many profound thoughts and considerably enriched its century. Nineteenth-century Socialism was not only a product of the French Revolution, it was also in a way a reaction against the failure of the Revolution to realize its promises of

Freedom, Equality and Fraternity. Socialism represents the materialist and atheistic perversion of a theocratic idea. It aspires to achieve human happiness while setting limits to the liberating movement of the Renaissance. The French Revolution was based upon man's self-affirmation; but its sad history discloses the interior contradiction which would not permit either the real liberation or realization of human rights, and which finally produces an inevitable reaction.

Fabre d'Olivier, an interesting French thinker, attempts to establish in his *Histoire Philosophique du Genre Humain* the existence of three mutually dependent principles in the history of human societies. These are necessity (*le Destin*), the Divine Providence (*la Providence*) and, finally, human freedom (*la Volonté de l'Homme*). In the French Revolution the principle of human liberty or the human will is actively engaged against that of Providence or the Divine. The reaction against the Revolution therefore represents the principle of necessity. Then *Le Destin* begins to assert its rights against human arbitrariness. Napoleon was the instrument of necessity in revolt against the human will. Necessity in all its terrible force swooped down upon the French Revolution and the orgy of human freedom and boundless human presumption which had torn man away from the higher principles. Its blow was the penalty humanist freedom had to pay for its false divorce of the natural from the spiritual man and its loss of all notion of the spiritual significance of freedom. Thus necessity reacts against presumption; but it is powerless to do anything against spiritual freedom.

The sixteenth-century Renaissance had been preoccupied with antiquity. That of the nineteenth century, on the contrary, was inspired by the Middle Ages, which offered a basis for the creative researches of the Romantic revival. The latter was likewise a manifestation of humanism, one that attempted to save human creation by enriching it from mediaeval sources, which were now made to provide spiritual nourishment for it. It attempted to restore human creation to the high level of the Christian consciousness and thus prevent its decay. This communion with mediaeval ideals was also a feature of the later nineteenth century, which witnessed the development of a mystical movement in certain centres of spiritual culture.

Humanism, it is clear, reaches its highest point of development and creative effort when it maintains itself on a purely human level as, for example, in the German Renaissance and the personality of Goethe. This was the last manifestation of a purely ideal humanism. Herder regarded humanity as the supreme goal of history; but he was the last real humanist. For him man was the first being to realize his freedom and to stand upright. Man was a king in his freedom. In Herder's humanism man was still associated with the Deity. His humanism was religious, but his religion was humanist. For him man was a medium between two worlds. Man was born for immortality and his powers contain in them the elements of infinity. The education of the human species was the problem which preoccupied both Herder and Lessing, According to them man's goal lay in himself, that is, in humanism. Following upon the German revival of Herder, Goethe and the romantics, humanism suffered a profound change and lost its links with the age of the Renaissance. The nineteenth century opened with the crisis of humanism and the exhaustion of the Renaissance spirit. It disclosed the abyss of diametrically opposed principles.

CHAPTER VIII

THE END OF THE RENAISSANCE AND THE CRISIS OF HUMANISM: THE ADVENT OF THE MACHINE

We are now approaching my main theme, the end of the Renaissance and the crisis of humanism. The era we are now entering is for me synonymous with the end of the Renaissance period of history. It is, however, necessary to explain why the creative spirit of the Renaissance and the energy of modern history have exhausted themselves, and are being supplanted by another spirit. To grasp the essentials of this development, we shall have to consider the primal bases of the whole of the historical process as we have outlined it. It is founded upon the relation of the human spirit and its destiny to nature; and this constitutes its primary pattern.

We can establish three periods of man's relations to nature. First of all, there is the pre-Christian pagan period whose feature is the immersion of the human spirit in nature and its direct organic blending with it. This is the primal stage of man's relations to nature wherein his life is governed by an animistic conception. Secondly, there is the Christian stage comprising the whole of the Middle Ages and marked by the heroic struggle of the human spirit against the natural elements and forces. The human spirit becomes divorced

[150]

from nature and seeks refuge in its own inner depths; it tends to regard nature as a source of sin and subservience to the baser elements. And, finally, there is the third period which gives rise to a new attitude to natural life. But this latter must be sharply distinguished from that direct communion with nature which had existed in the earliest stage of world history.

The new attitude does not wage a spiritual war against the natural elements as had been the case in the Middle Ages; it is concerned, rather, to conquer and master the natural forces with a view to transforming them into an instrument of human aims, interests and happiness. This intention does not become immediately apparent during the Renaissance which, at the beginning, manifested itself pre-eminently in an artistic and scientific contemplation of the mysteries of nature. But gradually man's new attitude to nature asserted itself. The conquest and subjection of external nature brings about a change in human nature itself; and, by its creation of a new environment, modifies not only nature but man himself. Human nature undergoes a radical change. There is a transition from the organic to the mechanical type. A profound revolution takes place introducing a mechanical order of life in contrast to the organic life and rhythm which had governed man's relations to nature in the earlier stages.

The history of the Renaissance period, which extends over several centuries, does not strictly coincide with the 'Renaissance' itself. The sixteenth, seventeenth and eighteenth centuries constitute a transition period in which man may be regarded as free from the organic ties of life, but not yet subject to its mechanism. Human forces are liberated for creative action. Man had emerged from the depths of organic, communal and personal life, and had cast off the compulsory tie subjecting him to the organic centre. There was no new tie to replace the old; and the domination of the mechanical conception was still a thing of the future. This transition period, therefore, permitted the free play of human creative forces and was most rich in historical context.

What had happened then in the history of mankind? How are we to explain the fact that the whole order and rhythm of life had undergone a radical change? Why did the decline of the Renaissance, already apparent in the nineteenth century, become much more accentuated in the twentieth? I am deeply convinced that an unexampled revolution and crisis of the human species had taken place, one that cannot be recognized by such outward signs as had distinguished the French Revolution from year to year, a revolution that was, in fact, immeasurably more profound. I have in mind the changes associated with the introduction of machinery into the life of human societies. I believe that the triumphant advent of the machine constitutes one of the greatest revolutions in human destiny. We have not yet made a just estimate of its importance. The advent of the machine brings about a revolution in all spheres of life. It rips man away from the bowels of nature and changes the whole rhythm of his life. Formerly, an organic tie had existed between man and nature, and his communal life had been governed by a natural rhythm. The machine radically modifies this relationship. It steps in between man and nature; and it conquers not only the natural elements for the benefit of man, but also, in the process, man himself. It both liberates and enslaves him once again. If man had formerly depended upon nature and had, as a result, lived a meagre life, the invention of machinery and the resultant mechanization of life while in some ways enriching him yet impose a new form of dependence on him, a dependence, perhaps, even more tyrannical than that exercised by nature. A new and mysterious force, alien to both man and nature, now makes its appearance in human life; and this third, unnatural and non-human element acquires a terrible power over both man and nature. It disintegrates the natural human forms. It disintegrates and divides man so that he ceases to be the natural being he had been from time immemorial. It contributes most of all to bring the Renaissance to an end.

We arrive at a very strange paradox which provides a clue for many things in modern history. The age of the Renaissance opened with a research for perfect natural forms. This research was at the basis of both Renaissance art and science. There was also an active desire to regenerate and naturalize man's social life. A new era was thus inaugurated which supplanted the mediaeval struggle against nature. But the further development of the Renaissance and humanism disclosed the action of a principle which separated man still more irreparably from nature than had been done by the Middle Ages. Leonardo da Vinci, one of the greatest Renaissance geniuses in both art and science, illustrates its spirit perfectly in his works. He strove not only to discover the sources of perfect forms in art, but also to acquire an intimate knowledge of nature. He is among those responsible for the future mechanization of human nature and for the decline of the original Renaissance attitude to nature. He helped to separate man from the latter by introducing the machine between them and enclosing man in the artificial culture that was being created in this period.

[153]

Thus the Renaissance attitude to nature, which was limited to the discovery of the natural man, offered no guarantee against the process that was to separate man still further from nature and bring about his final disintegration and disruption as a natural being. Towards the end of modern history this process quickens its rhythm and produces an entirely unexpected result which contradicts the original Renaissance principles. The exhaustion of man's creative forces, which was the direct result of his rupture with the spiritual centre of life and his exclusive preoccupation with its periphery, is accompanied by the bankruptcy of humanism. The Christian image of man and his personality forged by the Middle Ages now begin to be shattered and disintegrated. The early Renaissance had encouraged spiritual creativeness, but, in the period that followed, natural man, becoming more and more isolated from his spiritual self, lost control of his personality and thus of an inexhaustible creative source. Man transferred his activities to the periphery of life and devoted his energies to establish the reign of the machine. The whole strength of man's creative forces had lain in the discovery of a deep, superhuman and divine principle animating his life. But once he had repudiated this principle and severed all connection with it, he shattered his own image and increasingly emptied himself of content and his will of purpose. This denial of the highest creative source and purpose, which are essentially superhuman, deprives creation itself of both source and object. The living sources of creation, both human and superhuman, dry up; the aim and object of creation, which are also superhuman, disappear; and the result is man's complete disintegration. For, when man follows the path of self-affirmation, ceases to respect the higher

[154]

principle and asserts his self-sufficiency, he exterminates and denies his true self according to the laws of an inexorable inner dialectic. To affirm himself and preserve the source of his creative energy, man must affirm God as well. He must affirm the image of God within him. For he can have no vision of himself if he has none of the higher Divine nature; he becomes the slave of the baser processes, disintegrating into the elements of his own nature and becoming the victim of the artificial nature of the machine he has conjured up into life, and these de-personalize, weaken and finally annihilate him. The affirmation of the human individuality and personality demand a tie with a higher divine principle. But when the human personality will admit no authority but itself, it disintegrates, allowing the intrusion of the lowest natural elements which consume it. When man will admit only himself, he loses consciousness of himself; for this necessitates the recognition of something outside of one's self just as being an individual necessitates the recognition of both another human personality and that of the Divine Being. This recognition makes us conscious of the human personality, while boundless self-affirmation, which admits nothing save itself, brings about man's immediate ruin. Humanism attacks both man and God. For man ceases to know himself when he knows of no higher being or other principles than those contained in the confined circle of his nature. Thus the denial of the higher principles makes man inevitably subservient to the basest infra-human principles. Such is the inexorable path followed by atheistic humanism in modern history. The individualism that knows neither bounds nor authority disintegrates individuality. The strange and mysterious tragedy of human destiny is apparent in the last achievements of modern history. On the one hand, we have the discovery of the concept of individuality which contributed a new and precious element to human culture; but, on the other, we witness its unparalleled disintegration. The individuality is doomed to perish as a result of its lack of restraint and limitation. The whole of humanist history therefore culminates in anti-humanism.

To illustrate this process by which humanism is transformed into its opposite, let us consider two great thinkers of the later nineteenth and twentieth centuries. These two men of genius, belonging to the opposite poles of human culture, the representatives of diametrically opposed and hostile spiritual orders, set their imprint with equal power on the destinies of mankind. The one influenced most the individual heights of spiritual culture; the other the masses of mankind and their social environment. I mean Frederick Nietzsche and Karl Marx. These two men, who have nothing in common, mark nevertheless the end of humanism and its transformation into anti-humanism. In them human self-affirmation becomes, though on an absolutely antithetical plane, synonymous with the denial of the human image. In Nietzsche, who is both the incarnation of humanism and also the victim of its sins, humanism culminates in the individual. His destiny illustrates the penalty paid by modern history as a consequence of the false premiss on which humanism had been based. With Nietzsche humanism reaches the end of its stormy and tragic history. This is clear from the words of Zarathustra, 'man is a shame and disgrace and should be transcended.' Nietzsche achieves this, and the transition from humanism to anti-humanism, through his idea of the Superman. Thus humanism at the peak of its development culminates in the idea of the Superman, in whose name it repudiates man as a shame and disgrace. It is the repudiation of man, the value of the human image, and the undeniable significance of the human personality. Nietzsche denies what was the deepest source of Christian revelation, namely, the undeniable significance of man's soul. For Nietzsche man is but a transitory thing, the means of bringing a higher being into the world; he is completely sacrificed to the idea of the Superman. For Nietzsche humanism is the greatest obstacle in the way of the Superman's affirmation. And thus a cleavage is brought about in the destiny of humanist individualism.

After Nietzsche humanism is no longer possible. He had laid bare all its contradictions. And thus European humanism, the intermediate reign of humanity pure and simple, meets its death on the peak of spiritual culture. The humanist arts and sciences are discredited. Nietzsche had opened a new spiritual era whose thought is tinged with religious mysticism. The humanist ideal is no longer tenable, and its culture is repudiated or set aside. Nietzsche's tortured life was synonymous with the decline of humanism; but he was still obsessed by a passionate yearning for the Renaissance. He regretted the exhaustion of its forces which he felt in himself; and that explains his idealization of Caesar Borgia. Describing this Renaissance hero, he tried to revive the exhausted Renaissance forces and prepare the ground for a new Renaissance. But his creative individuality and genius symbolized not the revival but rather the crisis and end of the Renaissance. For, although Nietzsche had reached the extreme height of daring in his passionate and rebellious affirmation of the creative individuality, the human image in him grows dim and faint. In its place we are given the mysterious and poignant image of the Superman, whose features are only faintly suggested, but who brings a sort of authentic religious hope of a higher state while, at the same time, holding out the possibility of an anti-Christian, atheistic and satanical religion.

Karl Marx, who was gifted with an extraordinarily fine mind and great powers but did not in the least resemble the creative personality of Nietzsche, also symbolizes the decline of the Renaissance and the crisis of humanism. Nietzsche had symbolized the self-renouncement of both the individual and humanism. Marx, on the other hand, demonstrates the collective disintegration of humanism and man's image. Like Nietzsche, he can find no satisfaction in the purely human, in the affirmation of man and his individuality. And he, too, takes refuge in the non-human and superhuman. But Marx's non-human and superhuman consciousness differs from that of Nietzsche. Like him, Marx denies the value of the human individuality and personality, and of the Christian doctrine of the soul and its undeniable significance. For him man is but an instrument, paving the way for the advent of non-human or superhuman principles in whose name he declares war on humanist morality. And thus he preaches cruelty to man and one's next of kin in the name of the establishment of a non-human and superhuman reign of collectivism. The doctrines of Marx and Nietzsche, though deeply opposed in many respects, bear a formal resemblance to each other; they represent the two avenues of escape open to the humanist crisis, the two means of transforming humanism into anti-humanism, and, ultimately, the two forms of man's self-destruction. Marx is the child, too, of human self-affirmation, of man's presumption and rebellion against God, of his affirmation that the human will is the highest of all. His doctrine denies every superhuman principle. And yet his philosophy is accidentally based upon Feuerbach's anthropology according to which man had become God and the mysteries of human nature religion.

This path of human self-affirmation and presumption, of the supremacy of the human will, was destined to bring about man's inner ruin. Like Nietzsche, Marx gives us the faint outlines of the future Superman and the non-human collective in whose name man himself is denied. Man is, however, the means and instrument by which this non-human collective will be established at the expense of his human liberty and dignity. The covenant of humanist morality had lost all its value for Marx. He qualified it as being merely the bourgeois morality of the Renaissance period of history, and he regarded the whole of human culture in the same light. The reign of the bourgeoisie had culminated in the proclamation of the Rights of Man. But it was destined to come to an end, to disintegrate and be superseded by a new non-humanist and non-human reign, which would have its own morality and culture, its own non-human art and science, in short, all the attributes of the newly born and terrible collective society. Nietzsche and Marx exhausted the possibilities of humanism; the former on the peaks of culture, the latter among the masses in the plain below.

A knowledge of what these two great men contributed to the development of the last decades of European and Russian life should throw a great deal of light on the essential process of humanist evolution. Marx finally repudiated the heritage of the Renaissance. Unlike Nietzsche, he had no sympathy for its creative forces and no desire to revive its glories. He declared war against all its primal sources and proclaimed its whole creative effort to be no more than a superstructure founded upon the economic basis of man's exploitation of man. But the Renaissance had finally spent itself and provoked the crisis of humanism. Its joyous and exuberant play of forces disappears without hope of return. In the succeeding period the image of both man and nature is deeply shaken as a result of the changes brought about by the advent of the machine. The changed background in Marx is directly related to this event which had particularly struck his imagination. It had, indeed, impressed Marx so much that he made it the foundation of his philosophy and revealed its infinite significance for the human destiny.

The spread of democracy is closely connected with the decline of the Renaissance to which it dealt a death-blow. For the Renaissance and humanism were essentially aristocratic. The democratic vulgarization of culture and its propagation among the masses modifies the whole conception of life and makes the *via media* of humanist aristocratic rule impossible. This process changes the direction of human history. During the humanist crisis, which marks the end of modern history, man experiences a profound sense of isolation and abandonment. In the Middle Ages he had been a member of some guild or corporation, and had been conscious of his participation in some greater organism of which he was a part and with which his destiny was intimately linked. This state of affairs, however, comes to an end with the development of modern history. Modern man has become isolated, a mere atom. His isolation inspires him with a feeling of inexpressible terror from which he seeks refuge in associating himself with some collective; for, otherwise, he is threatened with spiritual and material starvation. Thus the process of atomization gives birth by way of reaction to that of communion with a collective and the establishment of a new principle which shall rescue him from his isolation.

Man's self-consciousness at the beginning of modern history had inspired him with confidence in his boundless creative powers and his ability to create life through the medium of art and the infinite possibilities of his knowledge when applied to the mysteries of nature. But this self-confidence was eventually undermined and superseded by a consciousness of man's limitations as a creator. This process was accompanied, too, by schism and self-doubt. Thus man's self-confidence and self-affirmation have become collective rather than individual. The admission of his limitations and the denial of anything supernatural assures finally the triumph of positivist philosophy. By his self-affirmation and the denial of anything superhuman, man only succeeded in undermining his own consciousness of power. This is the paradoxical antithesis at the basis of humanism in modern history.

Humanism started on its career by affirming the power of man's knowledge and art to regenerate human society. But man's absorption in himself to the exclusion of all superhuman elements was ultimately to lead him to doubt the extent of his powers. In this form, the humanist crisis has its roots far back in the past. It was manifest in all spheres of human culture. The disintegration had set in. Let us take the sphere of knowledge as an example. The Renaissance man had given himself up to the research for knowledge ecstatically and full of faith in his ability to solve the mysteries of nature. Catholic dogma seemed to impose certain limits to man's knowledge; and modern man accordingly attempted to overcome this obstacle. In natural philosophy, in the sciences, in various current forms of magic, the Renaissance man felt his capacity for knowledge to be infinite, and did not stop to reflect upon or doubt the means at his disposal. But this assertion of his human powers sapped the high religious and spiritual foundations upon which knowledge had rested in the Middle Ages as well as in the pre-Christian world; and this in turn helped to undermine his means of attaining to it.

Then we have the reign of speculative philosophy which finds a masterly expression in Kant, in whom the symptoms of the declining Renaissance are well illustrated. Kant's world is no longer that of the Renaissance; it lacks the joy of both knowledge and its infinite perspectives. It is bounded by the speculative awareness of the limitations of knowledge and the necessity of its formal justification. This self-consciousness in the sphere of knowledge is a sure sign that the Renaissance spirit had exhausted its thirst for knowledge. The Renaissance energy had given an impetus to a great development in science in the persons of Galileo and Newton. But Kant takes the mathematical sciences as the object of his speculative criticism. This critical work, which begins to doubt man's infinite power of knowledge, precipitates a conflict with anthropology and the humanist principles of knowledge; and this dispute reaches a particularly acute stage in the work of Cohen and Husserl. These philosophical currents, in their dispute with anthropology, even go so far as to affirm that man is an obstacle to knowledge. One of the representatives of this school has made the following strange and, at first sight, ridiculous statement, namely, that man's subjective presence constitutes the greatest obstacle to philosophical knowledge. This implies, of course, the existence of a non-human act of knowledge purged of all 'humanist' elements. But these positions are really symptomatic of the bankruptcy of the humanist conception of knowledge.

This tendency may be observed even more vividly in the positivist doctrine which, though it has now exhausted its force, played an important rôle in the nineteenth century. Positivism, too, was an anti-Renaissance movement illustrating the crisis of humanism. But Auguste Comte, who is an even more remarkable thinker than his doctrine might lead us to suppose, showed a marked tendency to revive certain mediaeval elements. His Positivism was, in fact, based upon certain mediaeval conceptions and represented an attempt to put an end to the free 'Renaissance' play of man's creative forces in the spheres of knowledge, spirituality and society. Auguste Comte wished to overcome what he called the 'anarchy of the mind', which was the direct outcome of the French Revolution. He would have liked to supersede the critical type of life by the organic, that is, by a spiritual centralization and the enforced subjection of modern man to a spiritual authority on the mediaeval model; and he would have liked to put an end to the individual will and the independent manifestation of creative forces. Like Marx, he would have liked to subordinate life to a certain binding authority with which he himself proposed to invest an erudite aristocracy. Auguste Comte, in fact, desired to establish a positivist religion to which he adapts various forms of the mediaeval Catholic cult. Thus he would have positivist Saints, a positivist calendar, the religious regimentation of life, a hierarchy of scholars, in brief, a revival of Catholicism without God. His system is therefore based upon Catholicism, but he replaces belief in God by that in a Higher Being—mankind, in the name of

[163]

which a cult of 'the eternal feminine' is created. Auguste Comte even erects an altar to this being in his home.

But this only serves to demonstrate how little positivist invention can affect man's religious nature. This partial revival of the mediaeval spirit marks the decline of the free individualism of the Renaissance period. The limits Positivism sets to man's knowledge are in direct opposition to the Renaissance spirit. The Utopian Socialism of Saint-Simon illustrates the same tendency. It represents a profound reaction against the French Revolution, eighteenth-century philosophy and liberal humanism as a whole. The atheistic religions of both Auguste Comte and Saint-Simon have nothing in common with the Middle Ages. And yet the latter attacks the critical work of the age of enlightenment and the French Revolution, and in its place would set up a system analogous to mediaeval theocracy. Both Auguste Comte and Saint-Simon had an equal esteem for Joseph de Maistre, who embodied the mediaeval revival of the nineteenth century. They were both determined to achieve a spiritual victory over individualism.

The decline of the Renaissance is also apparent in political life, where we may observe an interesting development. Modern history up to the time of the French Revolution, and even following it, is distinguished by the rule of a humanist monarchy. The reign of Louis XIV was essentially humanist. His famous dictum, 'L'état, c'est moi', was but an act of humanist self-affirmation. The whole style of the absolute monarchy under Louis XIV and the other monarchs of the seventeenth and eighteenth centuries was that of humanist self-affirmation. But the French Revolution replied to it by the self-affirmation of democracy; the revolutionary people in its turn said, 'L'état, c'est moi', and identified itself with the State. Thus one humanist self-affirmation was set up against another. Humanist democracy was an answer to humanist monarchy. In this way, when man repudiates his superhuman sources and affirms exclusively human principles, an inner process of revolution is set up which must inevitably lead to the ultimate humanist stage, that of revolutionary democracy. The French Revolution was the classical form assumed by this process in the West; but the fall of Tsarist absolutism was also the result of extreme human self-affirmation in the reign of Nicolas II, which was bound as a reaction to produce a revolutionary self-affirmation. And that was the penalty paid by Tsarism for its human self-affirmation.

Thus Renaissance states fall into two categories: into humanist monarchies and democracies. The Renaissance, too, favoured the development of nationalism, which converts the state into a closed national organism. But the period we are now entering is synonymous with the crisis of the Renaissance type of state. The humanist monarchy had in the course of its development been supplanted by humanist democracy; and we are now on the threshold of a period in which the foundations of both these institutions will be profoundly shaken, revealing the action of secret non-human principles of revolt against both these aspects of humanist government. The European states as well as Russia are now facing the critical moment of their destinies. The West is in the throes of the crisis of humanist democracies and their no longer creditable parliamentarianism and quantitative mechanism.

This crisis, of course, has a long history. The mechanical defects and inner instability of this order as well as the doubtful validity of humanist principles had made themselves felt long ago. It was apparent that another organic principle was expected to replace them. It was no accident that doctrines like that of corporative representation, which implies a certain revival of mediaeval principles, should again become current. This doctrine is based upon the idea that society should be composed not of atoms, but of organic corporations analogous to guilds and having their organic system of representation. In some respects this constitutes the revival of the mediaeval guild system upon a new foundation. It is the result, of course, of the crisis of parliamentary government which in reality satisfies nobody. The idea of corporative representation contains a healthy seed. All the great states to-day are pursuing an imperialist policy, which encourages the will to power and domination and thus undermines the foundations of the humanist national state. It contains also the elements of a superhuman principle. But this latter is also to be found in the modern type of collectivism.

The decline and crisis of humanism are likewise manifest in the sphere of moral life. There can be no shadow of doubt that we are living in an epoch marked by the bankruptcy of that humanist morality which had been the guiding light of modern history. But the close of the nineteenth and the beginning of the twentieth centuries demonstrated its final collapse. The Great War in particular, and its lasting consequences, dealt a death-blow to its illusions. But the ground had been prepared long before. Nietzsche had, of course, contributed to shake its foundations by revealing its latent contradictions. Its commandments were finally discredited by the current of spiritual philosophy which derived from Nietzsche and which no longer considered man, his interests, happiness and necessities, as the fundamental problem. The bankruptcy of humanist morality is apparent in other spheres. Thus the revolutionary and anarchic conceptions, though deriving from humanist sources, only help to hasten the process of humanist disintegration. The religious and mystical currents of the end of the nineteenth and beginning of the twentieth centuries contributed also to shake the humanist foundations by attributing a superhuman purpose to morality and thus denying the independent character of human principles. The intermediate reign of the Humanities of which Herder spoke comes to an end. Herder had taught that humanism was the highest aim of universal history. But it is only possible given a certain mean, and the non-disintegration into fundamental strata. Its sway in the upper strata of culture is possible provided that the problem of ultimate destiny has not yet become the preoccupation of human consciousness and that culture has not disintegrated into antithetical principles. The humanist period of history is based upon the principle of measure. It favours the efflorescence of culture. But as soon as the ultimate teleological problem is raised, the conception of culture transcends human limits and introduces an antithesis. The intermediate humanist reign then draws to its close. Nietzsche marks its end because he raised the ultimate problem. Marx, too, helps to close the humanist period of history by posing the social problem. Humanist religion likewise disintegrates when confronted by the ultimate problems for which the humanist reign offers no solution.

I have already referred to the highest point reached by humanist culture in Goethe before it had repudiated the divine principle. Goethe's humanism was based upon religion. In him the divine and human elements were harmoniously blended. But his art and knowledge, for all their greatness, did not achieve an ultimate consummation. His consciousness was neither apocalyptic nor preoccupied with the ultimate destinies of both man and the world. His life symbolized the flower of human creation before the dawn of a catastrophic interpretation of universal history. It constitutes, in fact, the high achievement of humanist creation. Following his authentic humanism, illuminated by the clear image of nature, the humanism of the later nineteenth and twentieth centuries becomes more and more of a shadow of its true self. The volcanic eruption of historical forces had begun with its accompaniment of disruption, division and catastrophes. No return is possible to humanist morality, art or science. An inexorable catastrophe had befallen man and afflicted his destiny. His sensibility is disrupted,—the inevitable result of the passage from man's self-affirmation to his self-denial, and of his divorce and isolation from natural life. Such is the terrible revolution which has, in the course of a century, sapped the foundations of modern history and inaugurated a new era.

CHAPTER IX

THE END OF THE RENAISSANCE AND THE CRISIS OF HUMANISM: THE DISINTEGRA- TION OF THE HUMAN IMAGE

First of all, I should like to consider Socialism as an aspect of the Renaissance crisis. Its significance cannot be underestimated, for it plays an important part in the life of the second half of the nineteenth and beginning of the twentieth centuries. It affects not only the economic life, but also the destiny of European culture whose inner processes it reveals. I therefore propose to examine Socialism as an integral whole, as a spiritual manifestation, and not as a specifically economic factor. Its mainsprings are deeply opposed to those of the Renaissance. The essential feature of the latter had consisted in its free display of exuberant human creative energy. Socialism, on the other hand, is based upon insufficiency and want rather than plenty. It manifests itself not in a free play of creative energies but in their subordination to a compulsory principle. It once again imposes upon free man the straight-jacket of an organized and regimented life. It is, in fact, the antipodes of the individualist ideal. Nevertheless, the conditions that gave rise to both Socialism and individualism have a great deal in common.

Socialism, I believe, is the outcome of the disintegration of human society and communal life, and of man's isolation

[169]

produced by the extreme development of individualism. The terror of abandonment and isolation in face of destiny, and the lack of all communion with other people, incite man to re-establish some form of communal and compulsory life. Socialism therefore springs from the same conditions as produced individualism, that is, the atomization of human society and the historical process. Thus, while the Renaissance had developed the individual, Socialism lays the foundation of a new mechanical collective society which subordinates everything to its own ends. The rise of such a collective society upon the ruins of an atomized society denotes the end of the Renaissance and the beginning of a new era in the life of human societies.

Socialism brings the free creative life of the individual to an end. The Hellenic principle of culture is relegated to a secondary plan, while the Judaic tends to become predominant. The advent of Socialism as a new force in European culture, its triumph and extension, imply a process of enslavement in every way antithetical to the process which had inaugurated modern history. This process of enslavement is in some respects analogous to that going on in the age of Diocletian and the early Middle Ages. Thus Socialism, although it is more progressive and revolutionary, has many affinities to the processes that were taking place in the decadent period of the ancient world.

Socialism contains a reactionary principle which is directed against both the Renaissance and the French Revolution stages of man's liberation, that is, against the whole of modern history. It is very important to establish this fact in order to understand the process we are now investigating. The Socialist idea has become a magnet not only for Russia, but also for Europe as a whole, which is bound to be affected sooner or later by the socializing processes. These latter are essentially a reaction against modern history which liberated the individual. They are accompanied by self-denial on the part of the individual; by escape from self and a search for a new communion, a new congregation and semblance of the Church. Socialism implies the subordination of all spheres of social life to an obligatory authority. The foundations of nineteenth-century society had been based upon contradictions. This had made it unstable and provoked a reaction. Neither humanism nor individualism could solve the destiny of human society, and both were destined to disintegrate. The Renaissance ideal of a free man was superseded by the anti-Renaissance ideal of a new organism or rather mechanism, which imposed its oppressive sway upon everything.

Anarchism is another aspect of the decline of the Renaissance. Its spirit is essentially anti-Renaissance. It appears to be a doctrine animated by an urge for liberty and the self-affirmation of the human personality. It is not, however, a doctrine of plenty, but one whose origins can be traced to the instincts of hatred and revenge. It is based upon the law of retaliation and the hatred of the past, of ancient culture and all history. It does not know the joy of exuberant Renaissance creation; its revengeful nature based upon want and suffering is essentially anti-Renaissance in spirit. Anarchism is therefore not by nature creative. Nor can positive creation be expected of an avid, malicious and revengeful negation. Anarchism neither knows nor can know the joy of free exuberant creation. Thus, like Socialism, it represents a departure from the Renaissance spirit.

Anarchism gives rise to an extremely interesting denial of

[171]

liberty. It affirms a freedom which inwardly devours and consumes itself. This is not a freedom that inspires the joy of a creative personality as does the freedom of idealist humanism. It is rather a limited, gloomy and torturing freedom in which the human individuality withers and perishes, and freedom becomes compulsion. And, ultimately, the majority of anarchist doctrines tend to affirm various forms of collectivism or communism. Such are the programmes of Bakunin and Kropotkin. I personally have no doubt that Anarchism is but another aspect of the exhaustion and decline of the Renaissance spirit. Neither its values nor morality are humanist in the sense in which the latter was understood by Herder, Goethe or Humboldt. It represents ultimately a reaction and revolt against culture, a repudiation of the inequalities and sufferings implied in it together with its high achievements in the name of an egalitarianism that levels and sweeps away all ascending values. This reactionary tendency of both Anarchism and Socialism is an outstanding feature of the humanist crisis.

The symptoms of Renaissance decadence are particularly clearly revealed in the various directions pursued by modern art. This decadence had already set in a long time ago. It is evident in Impressionism. And, in fact, all analytical-disintegrating currents in art are anti-Renaissance in tendency. Futurism in all its forms, however, marks the final rupture with the Renaissance tradition and, thus, with antiquity. All these modern artistic currents denote a profound disintegration of human forms, the shattering of the integral human image and a divorce between man and nature. The search for a perfect nature and perfect human forms had been the motive power of the Renaissance and constituted its tie with antiquity. Futurism is synonymous with the end of man as the greatest theme of art. It both eliminates and disintegrates man in art, which becomes a confusion of elements. The realities of the world lose their individual aspect. Man becomes dissolved in a welter of objects, lamps, divans, streets, which disassociate him as an entity and disintegrate both his image and inimitable countenance. Thus man becomes immersed in the surrounding world of objects. The austerity of forms, which had been the foundation of the pictorial art and had inspired the creations of modern man, is now violated. This profound rupture with antiquity and the Renaissance may be studied in the interesting Cubist works of an artist like Picasso. In them we see the process of disruption and disintegration, the disassociation of integral human forms and man's dissolution into component parts in an attempt to penetrate deeper into man's nature and discover the elementary forms making up his composition. Renaissance art offers an integral interpretation of human form. Nature was the model for these divinely created forms; and the imitation of antiquity only strengthened this view. The art of Picasso, on the other hand, breaks with both the ideal of nature and antiquity. It no longer seeks for the perfection of the integral man. It has, in fact, lost the faculty of integral interpretation and only strips off layer after layer in order to lay bare the inner structure of the natural being; or, penetrating ever deeper, it unearths the images of real monsters which are so vitally expressed in Picasso's canvases. It may be said of the Futurist currents in art that, though less significant than Picasso's painting, they go still further in the process of disintegration. When pieces of paper, newspaper advertisements, or objects extracted from a dustbin are inserted into pictures,

[173]

then it is finally patent that the process of disintegration and de-humanization has reached its climax. The human and every other natural form perish and disappear.

This disintegration of the human form is also a feature of the work of Andrei Biely.[1] His work, indeed, has many affinities to Futurism, although it is more significant than the work of most Futurists. It represents a profound rupture with the ancient traditions. In Biely's work in general, and in his remarkable novel *Petersburg* in particular, man becomes merged with a cosmic infinity, and the human forms distinguishing him from the world of objects are upset and confounded. We are faced with a process of de-humanization in which man becomes indistinguishable from the elementary spirits of cosmic life. Such are the anti-humanist principles underlying Biely's work. He carries on this process of human disintegration on the peaks of modern art. And thus, in the last fruits of his creative genius, modern man arrives at a negation of his own image. As an individual man ceases to be the theme of art and becomes immersed in social and cosmic collectives.

The anti-humanist principle may also be detected in other branches of culture. Modern Theosophy is both anti-Renaissance and anti-humanist. This becomes evident when we consider its doctrines. Its occult teachings, for example, subordinate the individual to a cosmic hierarchy of spirits. Man ceases to play the capital but isolated rôle that was his during the humanist period of history; he now finds himself on another cosmic plane, and subject to the influence of demons and angels. This feeling of subservience to cosmic hierarchies

[1]Andrei Biely (1880-1934), Russian poet, critic and prose-writer, who created a reputation for 'obscurity' by his 'Joycean' verbal experiments. The bulk of his work has not been translated.

induces a state of mind which makes the free play of human creative forces neither possible, justifiable nor admissible. Rudolf Steiner's occult teaching apportions man no central or exclusive place in the general hierarchy. According to it, man is but an instrument of cosmic evolution, the product of various cosmic forces and the point of intersection of the various planetary revolutions; in brief, man is the reflection of world evolution. Thus the term Anthroposophy is not really applicable to Steiner's teaching.

The anti-Renaissance character and structure of this type of doctrine are perfectly obvious. If we compare Steiner's theosophy with that of Paracelsus, the opposition between the two spirits will clearly emerge. Paracelsus was inspired by a full creative joy in penetrating the mysteries of nature and ravishing its innermost secrets. Steiner, on the other hand, lacks this creative joy; he insists on the painful process of human discipline which ultimately leads man only to the discovery of his dependence on the cosmic hierarchies. Man would seem to have lost all free will and feels, instead, the oppression of the life process, its immeasurable difficulties and disenchantment with modern history. And this feeling is characteristic of all the social and cultural manifestations of our time.

The religious and mystical movements of the nineteenth and twentieth centuries were a reaction against both positivism and materialism, but they themselves proved to be antihumanist in tendency. They represent a passionate research for spiritual authority and an admission that the life of free uncontrolled creative activity is no longer possible. They display a marked tendency to fall back upon mediaeval spiritual sources as a reaction against the principles introduced by the Renaissance. Great freedom of mind, too, was an im-

[175]

portant contribution of the latter; but it failed to maintain itself for long. Unbounded freedom had ultimately the effect of exhausting man's mental forces and making him repudiate his free achievements in modern history.

The crisis of culture and creation reaches its climax in the last few decades, when a multiplicity of symptoms testify to its urgent reality. One aspect of this crisis is an avidity to create accompanied by a creative impotence and incapacity as well as envy of the more integral cultural epochs. The revelation of certain inner contradictions inherent in the Renaissance also helped to make all creative efforts appear unsatisfactory and lacking in correspondence with the creative aim. The latter implies an urge to establish a new life and state of being; its realization, however, is an earthly process leading to differentiated cultural products. Instead of a new state of being, the result is limited to a poem, picture, scientific or philosophical book, a new form of law or ethics. All the products of human creation therefore bear the stamp of their terrestrial origin. Nor do they represent the higher life. Their forms do not correspond with the creative urge; and the creative result only leaves the creator deeply dissatisfied. This is the fundamental antithesis of creation. In our age, however, it has become particularly acute. I am even inclined to believe that this extreme consciousness of the crisis assailing creative activity is one of the deepest aspects of our age. The men of the Renaissance had created joyously, unconscious of the bitterness accompanying the non-realization of the creative aim. The great Renaissance masters experienced only the joy of creation and not the envenomed bitterness of a divided consciousness; and to this they owed their great mastery.

The chief artistic currents of our age bear the imprint of a deep inner dissatisfaction and torturing search for an escape from the vice that has gripped human creation. Great creative individuals like Nietzsche, Dostoievsky and Ibsen were both conscious of the tragedy of creation in the modern world and tormented by the impossibility of realizing the aim of their creative urge. All this, of course, is symptomatic of the decline of the Renaissance and the revelation of its inner antithesis which makes impossible any longer the free play of human creative forces in the spheres of either science, art, politics, ethics or jurisprudence. There is also a recrudescence of those barbaric elements which had lain concealed in the depths of human culture and which now prevent the further creative functioning of classical culture, art, science, political or ethical principles. Thus the intermediate reign of culture is brought to an end; its fabric is shaken by violent internal explosions and eruptions which indicate that the Renaissance has been discredited in all its forms. Europe, which had flourished so brilliantly for many centuries and had imposed its monopoly of high culture upon the rest of the world, would now seem to be entering a twilight epoch. Europe, having exhausted the possibilities of humanism, is heading towards a new form of mediaevalism. We are entering the night of a new Middle Ages, in which a new blending of races and cultural types is destined to occur. The importance of the philosophy of history lies in the clue it provides of the destiny awaiting the peoples of Europe and Russia; and also of the explanation it gives of the decline of humanist Europe and the nocturnal epoch of history lying ahead of us.

The end of modern history is characterized in all its

spheres and achievements by a deep sense of disillusionment. A consciousness of failure pervades its artistic, political and economic life. Man has failed to acquire a real power over nature. The proud dreams, which had given him wings during the Renaissance period, have come to nothing. His wings have been clipped and his pride humbled. His proud dreams of infinite knowledge and command over nature have only compelled him to realize his limitations and the impotence of science to solve the mystery of being. And speculative doubt only serves to undermine and diminish still further the power of science. Together with the growing uncertainty in the efficacy of man's knowledge it only frustrates the aims of philosophy. Recent gnosiological currents fail to attain to the ultimate knowledge of being and stop on the threshold of authentic philosophy. The latter, indeed, is suffering disintegration, having lost all faith in the attainment of integral knowledge by the means at its disposal. The crisis of philosophy is therefore the result of its impotence. It is accompanied, however, by a search for a religious basis,—a search that bears a close analogy to what was happening in the decadent age of the ancient world when philosophy became tinged with mysticism.

The same is true of art. The great art of the past would now seem to have been irretrievably lost. In its place we are offered a process of analysis and dismemberment. The advent of Futurist art is synonymous with the decomposition of the act of human creation. The same decomposition may be observed in the various social tendencies. Sensitive people are realizing more and more that neither empty freedom nor enforced fraternity can bring happiness. The ideals of the French Revolution have lost their glamour. The inner lack of content and the vanity of democracy are becoming daily more apparent, and a profound disenchantment is in store for both Socialism and Anarchism. Neither of these alternatives offers a satisfactory solution of man's social destiny. In brief, the final stage of modern history is coloured by a bitter sense of disillusionment in all its spheres. Man is to-day tormented by the disparity between the creative urge, energy and daring with which he had embarked upon modern history, and his final impotence either to realize his aspirations or to create. Thus man emerges from modern history not only deeply disillusioned, inwardly divided and disintegrated, but also creatively exhausted. Incapable of creating, he yet thirsts to create; this is the sign of both his impotence and the penalty inflicted on him for his self-affirmation and humanist refusal to submit himself to the supernatural, as a result of which his image disintegrates and his forces are dissipated. This suggests another comparison between contemporary history and the decadent epoch of the ancient world. In both cases a process of decomposition is accompanied by a nostalgia for a higher type of life and creation whose attainment is vitiated by a deep sense of impotence. From this it would seem possible to deduce that human history is subject to a periodical return of similar stages. I do not mean, of course, to imply that such stages repeat themselves, for nothing individual or historical can repeat itself; but rather that they offer a formal analogy which helps us to understand and compare our epoch with that which coincided with the birth of Christianity in the ancient world.

I have already attempted to explain the exhaustion of man's forces in modern history when dealing with the passage from the Middle Ages to the Renaissance. The Middle Ages with their asceticism, monasticism and chivalry had economized human forces and thus allowed their creative flowering in the age of the Renaissance. Humanism, on the other hand, repudiated both ascetic discipline and submission to supernatural principles. It dissipated and exhausted human forces, and thus undermined the authority of the human personality which had ceased to discipline itself and had, as a result, lost consciousness of itself, its identity and particularity. This fact may be observed in all contemporary cultural currents whether Socialist, Monarchical or Imperialist, as well as in art and the occult sciences. The human personality had been the great achievement of Christianity and European culture, but its disintegration is manifest to-day in every sphere of life. But once the personality has lost all idea and consciousness of itself, it seeks for a spiritual authority to restore its failing strength; for it feels that only exhaustion and the ultimate loss of freedom await it on the path it had followed since the Renaissance. And thus. it is eager to rediscover itself by submitting freely to some higher principle. The paradox holds true that man reveals and affirms himself only when he submits himself to a supernatural principle which becomes the content of his life. His repudiation of it, on the other hand, only leads to his perdition, for he is unable to discover a world other than his own human and confined world. The affirmation of the individuality postulates universalism. This is shown in all the achievements of modern history, in its science and philosophy, art and morality, politics, economics and technics. It demonstrates that humanist atheism leads to humanist self-repudiation or anti-humanism, and that freedom becomes compulsion.

[180]

Thus modern history draws to an end, giving place to a new era which I have called by analogy the New Middle Ages. And in order to integrate himself anew, man must submit himself once more to a higher power. Certain aspects of mediaeval asceticism must be revived in a new form in order to allow the human personality to reveal itself again, and in order that the Christian ideal so essentially a part of man's universal historical destiny might still prove a guiding light. We must now experience immanently what the Middle Ages had experienced transcendentally. The free self-limitation, discipline and submission to the supernatural on the part of man may still prevent the final exhaustion of human creative forces, and prepare the ground for a new Christian Renaissance which would dawn for an elect part of mankind on condition that the human personality had once more become strong and sure of itself. The Middle Ages had been founded upon the inner renouncement of the world, and in this had consisted its spiritual essence and strength. The renunciation of the world had given birth to the great mediaeval culture. The mediaeval idea of the Kingdom of God was that of dominating the world by its renunciation. The renouncement of the world by the Church led to the idea of the Church's universal power. This was the fundamental paradox discovered by such mediaeval historians as Aiken. I have already considered the fact that this idea could not be fulfilled. Nor had the idea of freedom been fully revealed to the mediaeval consciousness. The drama of modern history was inwardly inevitable. Modern man, however, in pursuit of his aim to dominate the world has become its slave. And having lost his entity in this way, he must now once more renounce the world in order to become its ruler and not its slave. Such is man's spiritual position to-day—at the close of modern history and on the eve of a new era.

Two paths lie open to contemporary man faced by a schism at the apex of modern history. He can either submit himself to the highest divine principles of life and thus strengthen his personality or he can become the slave and subject of non-divine, evil and superhuman principles. He is free to choose either path; and that is why universal history is the revelation of the Apocalypse. At the apex of modern history the human personality cannot bear to be the slave of either society or nature, and yet it is, in fact, increasingly the slave of both. Man attempted to master the natural elements by means of machinery and the development of his material productive forces, but in the process he has become the slave of both the machine and the social environment of his creation. The Capitalist system has clearly demonstrated this; and Socialism can only do so still further. Such is the tragic failure of modern history.

This failure, however, is neither altogether devoid of significance nor sufficient ground for an absolutely pessimistic interpretation of historical destiny. Modern history has its own inner significance if we conceive universal history, as indeed we should, as a tragedy. For if we are convinced that history has no immanent solution, then all its failures become imbued with a deep significance that transcends the fulfilment of a given aim in any particular historical epoch. The conception of a transcendental goal gives history a deep significance which it lacks when interpreted as the pursuit and fulfilment of immediate aims; for any such ultimate satisfaction would, however paradoxical it may seem, only make history meaningless. Its real significance lies not in a possible solution

at any given moment or period of time, but in the revelation of all its spiritual forces, contradictions and inner
tragedy; and, finally, in the withholding of the all-illuminating truth until the ultimate end. Such an ultimate
solution would throw light upon all the preceding historical
epochs, while any momentary solution of problems in a
given period could only be a partial solution. Nor does my
interpretation of history as a profound failure imply that it is
devoid of significance, for I consider its failure to be sacred.
It helps to demonstrate that the higher calling of both man
and mankind is super-historical, and that only this realization
can resolve the fundamental antitheses of history.

Russia, of course, occupies a unique position in relation to
the Renaissance and its decline. For Russia, although she had
never experienced the Renaissance, has been more acutely
aware of the humanist crisis than any Western European
country. This fact explains the peculiarity of her historical
destiny. The Russians have never either experienced the exuberant joy of Renaissance creation or been inspired by an
authentic enthusiasm for humanism. Russia's great literature, so far her most important contribution to the world,
is not Renaissance in spirit. There was only one moment in
her history when the glimmer of a Renaissance appeared
possible. That was in the age of Alexander I on which Pushkin had set the stamp of his creative genius. Pushkin did, indeed, represent a flash of the Renaissance spirit. But this epoch
of authentic culture proved to be but a brief interlude which
did not ultimately determine the destiny of the Russian
spirit.

Later nineteenth-century Russian literature did not develop on the lines laid down by Pushkin, but served rather

to demonstrate the impossibility of continuing his tradition. For Russian creation is on the whole a product of sorrow and suffering; and Russia's great literature is founded upon the thirst for expiating the sins of the world and bringing about its salvation. The joy of free exuberant creation was never the hall-mark of the Russian spirit. The lives of its geniuses prove this. Gogol's life and work were both profoundly sorrowful and tormented. So were the lives of Dostoievsky and Tolstoy. Their work as a whole is neither humanist nor Renaissance in spirit. Russian thought, philosophy, morality and politics all express a deep sense of anguish directly opposed to the joyous spirit of both the Renaissance and humanism.

Russia at the present time is experiencing the crisis of humanism in all the spheres of her communal and cultural life. Paradoxical as it may seem, Russia was destined to react against and give expression to this crisis in its most acute form. Dostoievsky in particular lays bare the contradictions inherent in the humanist ideal whose bankruptcy he demonstrates. Tormented by the problem of human destiny, which was the unique theme of his creative work, Dostoievsky revealed the profound tragedy underlying humanism. His whole dialectic is concerned to make its exposure as complete as possible. His own tragic humanism is very different from that expounded by the great European humanists.

It would, indeed, appear as if to Russian thought had been reserved the special mission of speculatively resolving the urgent European problems raised by the decline of the Renaissance and the crisis of humanism. Its constant concern with the goal of history makes this task peculiarly appropriate to it. Nor is it an accident that Russian speculation in the higher spheres of religious philosophy has always tended to be apocalyptic. This was the case of Chaadayev as well as Dostoievsky, Leontiev and Soloviev. In its metaphysical aspect therefore the Russian Revolution illustrates the bankruptcy of humanism which it interprets apocalyptically. It thus brings us nearer to the ultimate metaphysical problems of the goal and progress of history.

CHAPTER X

THE DOCTRINE OF PROGRESS AND THE
GOAL OF HISTORY

The notion of progress is fundamental for the metaphysics of history. It dominates speculation in Europe from the end of the eighteenth century. Yet it must not be thought of as an entirely original idea and peculiar product of the latest gains in human consciousness. Like all truths, it has ancient and profound religious roots. These appear in its intimate connection with the ultimate principles of historical life. We have already shown that the idea of progress is not to be confused with that of evolution. The idea of progress postulates a goal for the historical and its significant subordination to a teleological principle. It furthermore postulates a purpose independent of the historical process, one not situated within history nor connected with any given period of past, present or future, but detached from time and thereby qualified to elucidate the historical process.

This idea has ancient religious-messianic roots. It is the old Judaic idea of the messianic solution of history, of the advent of a Messiah who will solve the earthly destiny of Israel and, with it, that of all peoples. It is the ancient belief in the realization, sooner or later, of the Kingdom of God, the reign of perfection, truth and justice. This messianic and millenarian idea becomes secularized in the doctrine of progress, that is, loses its manifestly religious character and assumes one that is worldly and even anti-religious. It is not an exaggeration to say that for many people the doctrine of progress was a religion, that the religion of progress in the nineteenth century was professed by many who had fallen away from Christianity. An analysis of this idea of progress, with special reference to its religious pretensions, will reveal the fundamental contradiction that it involves.

The more recent tendency of human consciousness has been to undermine this idea of progress, dethrone its idols and submit it generally to the most searching criticism. The fundamental contradiction involved in the doctrine of progress, as laid bare by the metaphysics of history, resides in its relation to the problem of time, past, present and future. The doctrine of progress is first and foremost an entirely illegitimate deification of the future at the expense of past and present, in a way that has not the slightest scientific, philosophical or moral justification. The doctrine of progress is bound to be a religious faith, since there can be no positive science of progress. Such a science can only be one of evolution. The doctrine of progress is the 'herald of expectation', necessarily concerned with the 'revelation of the invisible', with the future. But this faith and expectation implicit in the doctrine of progress cannot solve the most tragic problem in the metaphysics of history, that of time. I have already referred to the capital importance of this problem in the metaphysics of history. I have endeavoured to show how time seems to decompose into its past and future and how this process of disintegration, disruption and dissolution is in fact an illusion. But the reality of this disruption is indispensable to the doctrine of progress. It postulates the solution of the

[187]

problems of universal history in the future and the coming of a time in the destiny and history of mankind when all historical problems and antagonisms will be resolved. This was the faith of Comte, Hegel, Spencer and Marx. But has such a superstition any justification? Is there any ground for such a belief? If so, is there any reason why it should be ethically welcomed? Is there any reason to rejoice in such an expectation? In fact the belief is groundless, except in so far as the latent and unconscious content of the doctrine is that old religious trust in the resolution of universal history, the trust, that is, in an end to the tragedy of universal history.

The resolution of this tragedy is the purpose of progress, but the nineteenth-century positivist doctrines of progress deliberately stifled and suppressed the religious element in this belief and hope. The theoreticians of progress opposed their faith and expectation to the religious type of these dispositions. But what is left of the idea of progress, once it has been emptied of its religious content? How can such a mutilated idea be inwardly accepted? For the positivist doctrine of progress simply states that in the torrent of time and generations whereby the destinies of human history are achieved, man advances steadily to some strange untrodden height, to some nobler and better state in relation to which all that has gone before is but a means and an instrument and not an end in itself.

In the light of progress every human generation, every individual, every epoch of history, are but the means and instrument to this ultimate goal of perfection, this ultimate humanity perfect in that power and happiness which are denied to the present generation. Both from the religious and ethical points of view this positivist conception of progress is inadmissible, because by its very nature it excludes a solution to the tragic torments, conflicts and contradictions of life valid for all mankind, for all those generations who have lived and suffered. For it deliberately asserts that nothing but death and the grave awaits the vast majority of mankind and the endless succession of human generations throughout the ages, because they have lived in a tortured and imperfect state torn asunder by contradictions. But somewhere on the peaks of historical destiny, on the ruins of preceding generations, there shall appear the fortunate race of men reserved for the bliss and perfection of integral life. All the generations that have gone before are but the means to this blessed life, to this blissful generation of the elect as yet unborn. Thus the religion of progress regards all the generations and epochs that have been as devoid of intrinsic value, purpose or significance, as the mere means and instruments to the ultimate goal.

It is this fundamental moral contradiction that invalidates the doctrine of progress, turning it into a religion of death instead of resurrection and eternal life. There is no valid ground for degrading those generations whose lot has been cast among pain and imperfection beneath that whose pre-eminence has been ordained in blessedness and joy. No future perfection can expiate the sufferings of past generations. Such a sacrifice of all human destinies to the messianic consummation of the favoured race can only revolt man's moral and religious conscience. A religion of progress based on this apotheosis of a future fortunate generation is without compassion for either present or past; it addresses itself with infinite optimism to the future, with infinite pessimism to the past. It is profoundly hostile to the Christian expectation of resurrection for all mankind, for all the dead, fathers and forefathers.

This Christian idea rests on the hope of an end to historical tragedy and contradiction valid for all human generations, and of resurrection in eternal life for all who have ever lived. But the nineteenth-century conception of progress admits to the messianic consummation only that unborn generation of the elect to which all preceding generations have made their sacrifice. Such a consummation, celebrated by the future elect among the graves of their ancestors, can hardly rally our enthusiasm for the religion of progress. Any such enthusiasm would be base and inappropriate.

The fundamental weakness of the idea of progress lies in its attitude to the insoluble problem of time. The only possible solution of universal history and its antithesis is in terms of a victory over time, over its disruption into past, present and future, over its disintegration into reciprocally hostile and devouring elements. The solution of the destiny of universal history involves the definitive conquest of time's corruptible nature. No doctrine of time admits of any such hope or purpose, either as a fact or as a problem. The theory of progress is not concerned with the solution of human destiny and history in timeless eternity, beyond the limits of history itself. It is concerned solely with a solution within the time torrent of history, a solution at a particular moment of the future which proves to be the assassin and devourer of the past. The idea of progress bases its expectation on death itself. Its promise is not of resurrection in eternal life, but of the incessant extermination of past by future, of preceding by succeeding generations. The all-resolving happiness will dawn at some moment of the future, but until then every moment is a disintegrated particle, the devourer and the devoured, the past devouring and being devoured by the future. The nineteenth-century doctrine of progress is no more than the temporary reflection of the nineteenth-century European consciousness, with all the limitations of its age. It corresponds to a given epoch and contains no absolute truth except in so far as its rationalizations have an unconscious principle, the ancient religious faith in an ultimate solution of human destiny and history.

The Utopia of terrestrial paradise and beatitude is closely connected with the doctrine of progress. But this Utopia is nothing more than a perversion and distortion of the religious faith in the coming of the Kingdom of God on earth, the grotesque rationalization of an unconscious millenarianism. Such a concept has been discredited in theory and rejected as unfeasible in practice. The Utopia of a terrestrial paradise contains the same fundamental contradictions as those involved in the doctrines of progress, in so far as it also postulates an ultimate perfection within time and the limits of the historical process. It looks forward to a solution of mankind's historical destiny within the closed circle of forces in which that history and destiny evolve, to the immanent solution in a perfect state of the tragedy of universal history. Based, like all theories of progress, on a false conception of time, it asserts unjustifiably that the problem of time is susceptible of solution in the future. The Utopia of a terrestrial paradise, imminent according to some, distant according to others, envisages a future state of perfect beatitude irrespective of the past. It asserts that the entire historical process has no other function than the preparation of this beatitude. The perfect earthly bliss of this fortunate race, sooner or later to crown the historical process, will expiate the pain and imperfection of all preceding generations.

Thus the Utopia of terrestrial paradise implies an absolute humanity within the transitory relations of terrestrial history. But there is no room in terrestrial reality, by its nature strictly confined and limited, for an absolute life. Yet the Utopia theory asserts that what has been impossible until now will not be so always, that an absolute and conclusive state will sooner or later crown historical relations. It affirms, not a transition from limited historical relations to some other plane of being, to some fourth dimension commensurable with the closed three dimensional world, but a fourth dimension of absolute life within the very framework of three-dimensional space. In this lie its fundamental metaphysical antithesis and essential instability. Instead of seeing absolute life as the transition from terrestrial to celestial history, it presupposes an ultimate solution of human destiny within the framework of terrestrial relations, a final integration of the three-dimensional world. It desires to humanize that absolute perfection and beatitude which can only be attained in the celestial reality and only contained in the fourth dimension.

This Utopia of a terrestrial paradise, characteristic of certain social doctrines and philosophies of history, has been submitted to a religious and metaphysical criticism from which it will not recover. The dual and profoundly tragic character of the historical process becomes increasingly manifest. There is no such thing in history as progress from good to perfect on a single plane of development, in virtue of which some future generation may exalt itself at the expense of all those that have gone before. There is no such thing in history as simple progress in human happiness. There is only progress in the tragic sense of the inner principles of being, of the good-evil, divine-demonic antithesis, of the principles of good and evil in collaboration. The fundamental significance of mankind's historical destiny resides in this antithesis and in its manifestation. If there has been any gain in human consciousness, it consists in a sharpened sense of this tragic antithesis at the core of human existence. Yet we may not assert a gradual growth of the positive at the expense of the negative, as the theory of progress would maintain. As history evolves, its antithetical principle becomes more and more complex. Even if we were to think of progress as an approximation to the absoluteness of divine life, it would still be false to conclude that the generation destined to emerge on the peaks of history would be assumed within the absolute as against all those other generations whose contact with the divine life is either negligible or to be understood as a mere means to the ultimate goal. It would be more correct to adopt the view of L. Ranke, that every generation is in contact with the Absolute and Divine and that it is precisely in this that the Divine truth and justice consist. What could be more unjust than a monopoly of the divine life and mysteries reserved for a generation at the apex of progress?

Nothing is better calculated than this view of progress to make us doubt the very existence of a Providence. A Deity refusing itself to all past generations, admitting to its intimacy only the last and perfect product of history, could only be thought of as a vampire, unjust and pitiless to the vast bulk of mankind. It is on these grounds that Ivan Karamazov repudiates God. But in reality there is no such Deity. Every generation has its own goal, its own justification, its own meaning, its own values, its own spiritual impulses whereby it approximates the divine life. It cannot be merely

[193]

an instrument and means of future generations. Is the nineteenth century any closer to God than its predecessors?

The doctrine of progress is further invalidated by another purely positivist-scientific criticism. When we examine the destinies of peoples, societies, cultures, we observe how they all pass through the clear-cut stages of birth, infancy, adolescence, maturity, afflorescence, old age, decay and death. Every great national society and culture has been subject to this process of decay and death. Cultural values are deathless, because culture contains a deathless principle. But the peoples themselves, considered as living organisms within the framework of history, are doomed to wither, decay and die as soon as their efflorescence is past. No great culture has been immune from decadence.

One of the most obvious objections to the theory of progress is the discovery of a great culture like that of Babylon, which flourished three thousand years before Christ and attained a pitch of perfection in many respects superior to anything of which the twentieth century is capable. Yet it died and vanished almost without leaving a trace. For a long time its existence was not even suspected. Only the more perfect instruments of archaeological research made it possible to unearth this culture and create the pan-Babylonian enthusiasm.

Such considerations have led so important an historian as Edouard Meyer to deny categorically the existence of human progress along a straight ascending line. There is a development only of distinct types of culture and succeeding cultures do not always reach the heights of those that went before. Such a conception is not necessarily pessimistic. There is no reason for making one's optimism, creative energies and prospects depend on the modified values of later generations.

There is no ground for the conviction that these are more authentic than those which obtained in the past. A little consideration will reveal the absurdity of supposing that the present generation (if one can call 'present' that which is in the act of disappearing) or the generations of fifty or a hundred years hence can make a more real and valuable contribution to the human consciousness than those which existed fifty, a hundred or five thousand years ago. Our habit of breaking up time into the past, present and future does not entitle us to endow the last with more reality than the first. From the standpoint of the present, the future is no richer in reality than the past, and our efforts should be with reference, not to the future, but to that eternal present of which both future and past are one. The past has no existence except in our memory; the future is not yet, nor is it certain that it will be.

In a sense it may even be argued that the past is more real than the future, that those who have departed from us are more real than those who have not yet been born. We assume a future rich in higher life and faculties which it is our function to prepare. This assumption, which should constitute the meaning, joy and vigour of life, has been perverted by the nineteenth century into one of the gloomiest prejudices of the religion of progress. Our real task is to break finally with the expectations, hopes and beliefs involved in this attitude towards the future. The faith and trust which raise us above the present moment into the dimension of a great historical destiny should inspire us to do away once and for all with the disintegration of time into present, past and future, and set up the true era of eternity. Our belief and expectation should tend towards a solution in eternity of human destiny, towards a perspective of life based not on a detached future but on the eternal and integral present. It is not our function to submit our contribution to the criteria of some future fragment of time. The corresponding generation will attend to that. But our function at every period, at every moment of our historical destiny, is to determine our relation to the problem of life and history in the terms and according to the criteria of eternity. Only when we have situated human destiny and history in the perspective of eternity will the future appear no more real than the past and the present no more real than either. For eternal time suffers no divisions. The rationalization of a disintegrated time undertaken by the religion of progress is a sin before eternity.

The heinous contradiction at the core of the doctrine of progress constitutes its essential instability and the spuriousness of its humanist hypothesis. The beginnings of modern humanism tended to turn man away from eternity and deliver him up to the material torrent of a disintegrated time. They could not therefore furnish a fruitful solution to the problem of human destiny and history. The humanist hypothesis was organized about an inner rottenness which was bound to appear sooner or later. It appears in what I call the crisis of humanism and the decline of the religion of progress. It is no longer possible to believe in the humanist progress. The illusion of progress, indispensable to the humanist structure, permeated the whole of the nineteenth century. The secular doctrine of progress, severed from its true religious origins, is simply an attempt to set up as a system and a logical theory the humanist hypothesis that man can be an authority unto himself, qualified to determine his fate by his own intrinsic energies and to dispense with the divine purpose and direction.

Because the doctrine of progress shows up the humanist hypothesis as false and illusory, it does not follow that humanism has made no positive contribution. I believe that humanism contains a positive principle of immense importance for the future destiny and history of mankind. It was necessary for man to pass through the humanist self-affirmation and self-sufficiency, to give free play to his energies in the practical application of this doctrine. The energies thus set free may not have led to any very positive results. Nevertheless the mere fact of their liberation will acquire enormous significance when mankind has passed from the humanist to that further phase of its destiny of which we, standing on the threshold, can have no knowledge. Every new religious confession particularizes the spiritual energy of human culture. The characteristic manifestations of the humanist period have a spirituality of their own.

History is in truth the path to another world. It is in this sense that its content is religious. But the perfect state is impossible within history itself; it can only be realized outside its framework. This is the fundamental conclusion of the metaphysics of history and the secret of the historical process itself. In its perpetual transition from one epoch to another, mankind struggles in vain to resolve its destiny within history. Disappointed in its expectations, feeling itself imprisoned within the circle of history, it realizes that its problem cannot be solved within the process of history itself, but only on a transcendental plane. The problem of history is determined by the nature of time. To solve it requires an inversion of the entire historical perspective, a transfer of attention to extra-historical considerations, to the urge of history towards super-history. We must admit within the hermetic circle of history the super-historical energy, the irruption within the relations of terrestrial phemonena of the celestial noumenon—the future Coming of Christ. This concept of the ineluctable end of history is at once the final conclusion and fundamental premiss of the metaphysics of history.

So long as we consider the solution of the historical process as immanent within the problem itself, as a product of the time torrent, we cannot fail to arrive at the most hopelessly pessimistic conclusions. Such an approach cannot possibly yield a general solution valid for all the problems of all the periods of history. Man's historical experience has been one of steady failure and there are no grounds for supposing that it will ever be anything else. Not one single project elaborated within the historical process has ever proved successful. None of the problems of any given historical epoch whatsoever has been solved, no aims attained, no hopes realized. This radical failure of the historical process, when we regard it as a whole, can only be interpreted as the failure to realize the Kingdom of God. To situate the Kingdom of God as a solution of human destiny within the historical process itself is tantamount to excluding its realization and even its preparation.

Examining specific periods of history and their respective problems, we feel them to be consumed with an inner disease and impotent to arrive at a solution. To consider only modern history, its profound failure is amazing. The Revolutionary ideal did not succeed, if we are to judge by the extreme disparity between its achievement and its intention. The impossibility of Revolution within the Christian world has been demonstrated. For the Christian world is a prey to a malignant disruption intolerant of the revolutionary integrity. Nor is it possible to inject the Christian content with a new antiquity. A similar failure befell the Reformation, whose great purpose of affirming religious freedom only resulted in the collapse of religion. Similarly, the French Revolution established the nineteenth-century bourgeois society in place of the liberty, equality and fraternity of its ideal. The contradictions pervading the French Revolution became more and more flagrant all through the nineteenth century, until its ideology was finally shown to be utterly false. The hope of liberty, equality and fraternity was overwhelmed by an unprecedented recrudescence of class distinctions and class hatreds. And it may be asserted with no less certainty that the same failure is in store for the major ideals and problems of our own epoch, and notably for Socialism, whose efforts at self-realization will probably be a capital element of the immediate future. These efforts will transform Socialism into something quite different from the socialists' ideal. They will activate profound human antagonisms in the face of which there can be no solution of the problem as stated by Socialism.

Nor will Anarchism, that rival of Socialism, prove any more successful. So far from realizing the boundless freedom that it proclaims, it can only plunge mankind in a still profounder slavery. The fact is that no single revolution has ever succeeded in breaking the bonds of history. One may speak of revolutions as capital events in the destiny of mankind, as phenomena of inner and inexorable determination subserved by all that went before, but the fact remains that they have never solved the problems with which they were confronted. This has always been and always will be the case. It is only the experience of historical failure itself that has proved fruitful, in the sense that the consciousness of humanity has thereby been increased. What go by the name of achievements have always belied the plans and hopes of their artificers. Revolution ends in reaction, whose function is to define the experience. And the reaction itself is more often than not reactionary in the worst sense, causing human society to regress. Thus the spiritual reaction at the beginning of the nineteenth century proved one of the most positive effects of the French Revolution. The spiritual revival to which it gave rise conferred tremendous importance on this period, but an importance that did not consist with the revolutionary purpose. The same might even be said of the great central key event of universal history, of that Christianity which inaugurated an era and determined the course of all that was to follow. For Christianity also was a complete and utter failure. The enemies of Christianity take a malicious pleasure in indicating this very fact as the capital objection against Christianity. They repudiate Christianity because it did not succeed on earth. This is a criticism capable of quite a different import and interpretation. It is true that Christianity shared the collapse of every other historical process. Two thousand years have not sufficed to realize the ideals of Christian faith and consciousness. They will never be realized within the framework of human time and history. They can only be realized by a victory over time, by the transition from time to eternity, by the triumphant passage from the historical to the super-historical process. But the failure of Christianity can no more be used as an argument against its higher truth than the failure of history can be taken to imply the aimlessness and emptiness of history.

[200]

The failure of history does not mean that history is devoid of necessity or relevance. Similarly the failure of Christianity does not mean that Christianity is not the highest truth. Historical success and achievement do not constitute a valid criterion of the true. The nature of history and all that it contains is such that nothing perfect can be realized in time. The profound significance of historical destiny and experience does not depend on any realization. It exists beyond the limits of history. The failure, so painfully clear within the framework of historical time and terrestrial reality, does not imply limitation and failure outside that framework. It rather goes to prove that the destiny of man reserves a higher realization for his potentialities than any to be achieved in his purely historical experience. The failure of the Reformation, of the Revolution and of all that is historical, is simply a proof of man's inner division and a promise of his integration in a higher and more absolute reality than that in which such failure is inevitable. To pervert the historical failure of Christianity into meaning the failure of the Christian spirit is to take advantage of a verbal ambiguity. The failure is not of Christian absoluteness and truth, which neither time nor hell can destroy, but simply the failure inseparable from material relations, from disintegrated time and terrestrial conditions. Nor is the failure of God, as the adversaries of Christianity maintain, but of man. And this failure of man means simply that man is destined to realize his potentialities in eternity, in conditions far more real than those which have so far hemmed in his efforts. To base a criticism of Christianity on its so-called failure is doubly revolting. For it was only when Christian men had betrayed the Christian truth that they began to slander Christianity and repudiate it as having failed. The failure was a consequence of the betrayal. Thus the criticism is doubly fallacious.

To create beauty in this world we must situate the real centre of mankind in another world. The most beautiful creations of mankind have been determined, not by purely terrestrial aims and relations, but by a purpose set up beyond the limits of the natural world. The urge of the spirit towards another world takes bodily form in this as the noblest beauty of which we are capable, a beauty, that is to say, symbolic and not realistic. The ultimate real can only be realized in the higher reality, but here it may be symbolized and shadowed forth. This is especially clear in the case of mankind's highest achievement, art, essentially symbolic in its most perfect forms. The symbol achieved by great art is that of the higher reality which is mankind's destiny.

When I spoke of celestial history as the prologue to terrestrial history and then examined the latter in the light of this conception, I based the entire development of the tragedy of human destiny on a double revelation—that of God to man and, inversely, that of man to God. The essential tragedy of existence lies in this free inner relationship between God and man, in the birth of God in man and of man in God, in the revelation of God to man and of man to God. The history of mankind is permeated through and through by this double flow of revelation between God and man. His creative works, his historical acts, are man's answer to God. But his final and most significant answer is his freedom. His freedom to reveal himself, his freedom to create, respond to God's longing for man. God desires a free creative daring in man. But in man's historical destiny, in the whole pattern of his acts, we find many deviations from the path of freedom to that of compulsion and necessity. All human history is full of such temptations, from a compulsory Catholic or Byzantine theocracy to compulsory Communism.

The path of freedom is difficult and tragic, more beset than any other with heroic responsibility and martyrdom. The paths of necessity and compulsion are easier, less tragic and less heroic. That is why the historical process shows so many derogations from the path of freedom to that of compulsion. This is true of the religious as well as of the secular experience. The temptation is superbly expounded by Dostoievsky in his *Legend of the Grand Inquisitor*. The Grand Inquisitor wishes to relieve men of the burden of freedom, so that they may all be happy. Mankind yielded to this temptation in the Inquisition and does so again in our own time in the religion of Communism, which is simply the doctrine of the Grand Inquisitor based on the fall from the path of freedom to that of compulsion, so that mankind may be delivered from the burden of its tragic destiny. This is the very essence of the historical drama, rooted in the conflict between the principles of freedom and compulsion, in the ceaseless supersession of the one by the other.

What is the essential significance of the historical process? Can any such significance be said to exist if we deny the doctrine of progress, repudiate the apotheosis of future generations and the steady triumph of the positive principle through more and more good, more and more light, to the perfect beatitude? It is not so difficult for Christian philosophy to answer these questions, since the Christian philosophy of history is essentially apocalyptic. Both the Evangelical Apocalypse and the greater Apocalypse of St. John are agreed in their symbol for the sacred destiny of history. The apocalyptic prophecy has reference to the consummation of history and to its all-resolving end. The metaphysics of history apply the light of apocalypse to that dualism which must control the future, to those positive Christian forces which must culminate in the Coming of the Christ together with those negative anti-Christian forces which must culminate in the coming of the Antichrist.

Antichrist is the problem of the metaphysics of history. He will come not as the old evil inherited from the dawn of human history, but as a new evil, the evil of a future age more terrible than that of the past. The future has in store an unprecedented battle between good and evil, God and the devil, light and darkness. The significance of history is in terms of these antithetical principles, in their tragic conflict and decisive clash at last. Antichrist will chain mankind to this false time, will load him with the chains of terrestrial relations, on this finite plane of being. This is the inner meaning of the apocalyptic symbol. But the fact that the future carries the growth of evil as well as of good, of the antichristian as well as of the Christian principle, need not alarm the Christian philosophy of history and does not invalidate the inner significance of history. For this is precisely the content of the Christian prophecy, whose assertion with regard to the historical culmination is thereby confirmed. Exoterically the Apocalypse is simply the expression in convenient symbols of the esoteric Apocalypse of the human spirit. Its scope is the world aeon, not the ultimate depths of being.

In conclusion I wish to restate my opening theme. I began with the prologue of celestial history and made it the basis of my analysis of terrestrial history. I must now return to a consideration of celestial history. History has positive significance only when it has a culmination. The entire metaphysic of history, as I have endeavoured to state it in this book, concludes in the inevitability of historical culmination. If history were an endless process it would have no significance. The tragedy of time would admit of no resolution, the historical purpose of no realization, since neither the one nor the other can consist with historical time. The destiny of man implicit in the origins of history involves a super-historical goal, a super-historical consummation of history in eternal time.

Terrestrial history must once again be integrated in celestial history, there must be no more barriers between our world beyond, as there were none in the depths of the past, before the dawn of life. Myths are an expression of this primordial confusion of celestial and terrestrial. Our world aeon is coming to an end, the membrane separating it from other worlds will burst like that of a ripe fruit. This is the symbolical interpretation of the Apocalypse. The bond of time is broken, the closed circle of terrestrial reality is invaded by the energies of a higher plane, the history of our world in time arrives together at its climax and its meaning. Just as any given day of our individual life is meaningless until we relate it to all the other days.

History is powerless to solve the problem of individual destiny, that problem which pervades the magnificent confession of Dostoievsky and with which is bound up the entire metaphysic of history. The problem of individual destiny admits of no solution within the historical framework, any more than does its tragic conflict with the destiny of mankind and the world at large. The problems of individual destiny and of its conflict with world destiny will only be solved when the world has attained to a higher reality and an integral time.

[205]

History is pre-eminently destiny, tragic destiny. And the tragedy of destiny, like all tragedy, must end in resolution. There can be no tragedy without catharsis. History is not an endless development in time, nor is it subject to natural law, precisely because it is destiny. This is the ultimate finding of the metaphysics of history.

Human destiny as expressed in historical time admits of no resolution within the historical framework. But the metaphysics of history teach that what is insoluble within the historical framework may be solved outside it. And this is the capital argument for the supreme reality of historical significance. For if history had no significance other than that which was intrinsic and natural to itself, it could be truly described as devoid of significance. To suppose anything of the kind is to burke the fundamental problem of time or to solve it in a manner that is fictitious, superficial and vain.

The conclusion of the metaphysics of history is relatively pessimistic in so far as it breaks with the illusory apotheosis of the future and refutes the doctrine of progress. On the other hand, it strengthens the hope and expectation that the tragedy of history will be ultimately resolved on the plane and in the perspective of eternity, of eternal reality. This is a deeper and more real optimism than the wretched and arid variety put forward by the doctrine of progress. The time has come for that inner adjustment which will rescue universal history from the exterminating time torrent, from its exile on the surface of that spirit to whose depths it belongs, and restore it to the perspective of eternal and celestial history. The time has come for its profound reintegration as a moment in the everlasting mystery of the Spirit.

EPILOGUE

THE WILL TO LIFE AND THE WILL
TO CULTURE

There exists to-day no theme more urgent for both knowledge and life than that of culture and civilization regarded from the standpoint of their relations and distinctions.
It is that of the destiny in store for us. And nothing preoccu-
pies man more than his destiny. The extraordinary success of
Spengler's *The Decline of the West* is due to the fact that it
posed the problem of historical destiny. In an age of grave crisis
and catastrophes, at the cross-roads of history, we are obliged
to ponder seriously upon the dynamics of cultural and national destinies. The hands of universal history are pointing
to a fatal hour, that of twilight, when it is time to light our
lamps and prepare for night. Spengler proclaimed civilization to be the doom of every culture. Death stalks in its train.

The theme is not new. It has long been part of Russian
thought, philosophy and history. The great Russian thinkers
of the past had already drawn the distinction between culture and civilization and had applied it to the relations of
Russia and Europe. Our slavophile consciousness had as a
whole been permeated with hostility not to European culture but civilization. The thesis of the 'decaying West' was
intended to illustrate the death of a great culture and the
triumph of a soulless and atheistic civilization. Homyakov,

[207]

Dostoievsky and Leontiev had a genuine veneration for the great European past, that 'land of holy miracles', with its sacred monuments and ancient stones. But Europe had betrayed and repudiated its past. An atheistic bourgeois civilization had established itself on the ruins of an old and sacred culture. The struggle between Russia and Europe, the East and the West, was represented as that between the spirit and religious culture, on the one hand, and a soulless atheistic civilization, on the other. It was believed that Russia would not enter upon the path of civilization, that it would follow a path and destiny of its own, and that it was capable only of a religious and authentically spiritual culture. This theme was very dominant in the Russian consciousness.

But was this theme foreign to the Occidental consciousness? Had Spengler been the first to consider it or had not rather the whole of Occidental thought tended in that direction? Nietzsche's speculation is the acute expression of this fatal presentiment. His longing for the tragic dionysic culture is peculiar to an age of triumphant civilization. All that was genuine in Occidental thought revolted against the triumph of Mammon and a soulless technical civilization at the expense of spiritual culture. The romantics had all been deeply if not mortally wounded by this triumph. Carlyle revolted with prophetic force against this spirit-slaying civilization. So did Léon Bloy in his ingenious unmasking of 'bourgeois wisdom'. French Catholics, symbolists and romantics all took refuge in the Middle Ages, that remote spiritual fatherland, which seemed to offer the only escape from the mortal *ennui* of triumphant civilization. This Occidental urge towards past cultural epochs or the exotic cultures of the East denoted a spiritual revolt against the final transition of culture into civilization, but one that was too refined, decadent and spiritually feeble. In face of the menacing non-being of civilization, men living in an age of cultural decadence are incapable of realizing authentic and eternal being. Instead, they seek refuge in the world of the remote past which nothing can revive or in that of the immobile Oriental cultures which are spiritually alien to them.

Thus the banal theory of progress is exploded. It had propagated the belief that the future was always more perfect than the past and that mankind was ascending in a straight line to higher forms of life. But culture does not develop eternally. It contains the seeds of its own destruction. It is based upon principles which inevitably transform it into civilization. And the latter is the death of the spirit of culture, the manifestation of quite a different state of being or non-being. But this phenomenon so typical of the philosophy of history demands definition. Spengler, however, provides no clue to the apprehension of its meaning.

2

Every culture in the process of flowering and becoming more complex and refined exhausts its creative forces and spirit. Even its aims change. It becomes increasingly concerned with the practical realization of power and organization of life along lines of superficial expansion. The efflorescence of the 'arts and sciences', the profound researches of refinements of thought, the finer impulses of creative activity, the visions of saints or geniuses, all these cease to inspire and be regarded as the true authentic 'life', which comes to be interpreted in terms of the will to the experience, power, enjoyment and mastery of it. And this brings with it the death of culture. In an age of cultural decline the desire to 'live', to construct and organize 'life' is particularly intense. An age of cultural efflorescence, on the other hand, imposes a certain curb upon the will to 'life'. When the greed for life spreads to the masses, then the higher spiritual culture, which is always aristocratic and based upon quality rather than quantity, ceases to be the goal. The latter is now sought in 'life' itself, in its experience, power and happiness. Culture loses its inherent value and therefore the will to culture dies out. There is no more will to genius and geniuses become rare. Disinterested vision, knowledge and creation are at a discount. Culture cannot always remain on the heights, but must inevitably descend and fall. It is powerless to sustain its high level of quality and the quantitative principle overcomes it in the end. Thus a social mutilation is effected by which the creative energy of culture is dispersed. And the decline sets in because culture is incapable of developing eternally or realizing the aims of the creators.

Culture is not the realization of a new life or state of being, but of new values. All its achievements are symbolic. It does not realize the truth, goodness, beauty, power or divinity of life. It realizes truth only in philosophical and scientific treatises; goodness in ethics and social commandments; beauty in poems, pictures, statues, plays, music or architectural monuments; divinity only in cult and religious symbolism. Its centre of gravity lies below and weighs down the creative act. Similes, images and symbols are all the means it has of communicating the new life or the higher state of being. The creative act of knowledge gives birth to the scientific work; the creative ethical act brings about the establishment of customs and institutions; the creative religious act establishes the cult, dogmas and symbolic structure of the Church which is but the similitude of the heavenly hierarchy. Where, then, is the 'life' itself? For culture does not seem to be able to achieve a real transfiguration. And dynamic energy within the crystallized forms of culture leads irreparably away from culture, to the experience and power of 'life'. And this constitutes the transition from culture to civilization.

Germany at the end of the eighteenth and beginning of the nineteenth centuries offers an example of the high efflorescence of culture; it then became famed as the land of 'poets and philosophers'. Few epochs have displayed as much will to genius. In the course of several decades the world was enriched by such geniuses as Lessing and Herder, Goethe and Schiller, Kant and Fichte, Hegel and Schelling, Schleiermacher and Schopenhauer, Novalis and all the romantics. Succeeding ages will look back with envy at this great age. Windelband, the philosopher of its decline, remembers this time of spiritual integrity and spiritual genius as a lost paradise. But had the age of Goethe and Kant, Hegel and Novalis, attained to the authentic higher 'life'? All evidence tends to show that everyday life in Germany was then poor, middle class and oppressed. Germany was weak, wretched and split up into minute states; the power of 'life' had nowhere been realized; and the cultural efflorescence affected only the highest strata of the people whose general condition was lamentable enough.

Let us now turn to the age of the Renaissance. Had this incredibly creative epoch realized the authentic 'life'? Nietzsche, the romantic, may seek escape from the civilization he hated in the delights of the authentic and mighty 'life' of the Renaissance; but that 'life' was imaginary. The everyday life of the Rennaissance was terrible and evil, and it failed to achieve the perfection of terrestrial beauty. The life of both Leonardo and Michael Angelo was one long torment and tragedy. And so it has always been. *Culture has always proved life's greatest failure*. An antithesis would seem to divide culture from the 'life' that civilization attempts to realize. When a mighty German state is finally established, Capitalism and Socialism accompany it; and its main efforts are directed to assert its will to world power and organization. But Goethe, the great idealists and romantics, great philosophy and art, will be missing from this mighty Imperialist and Socialist Germany. They will have been supplanted by technique, which has its repercussions even upon philosophical thought (in the gnosiological currents). Conquest is the method now applied in all spheres at the expense of the integral-intuitive apprehension of being. The mighty civilization of the British Empire holds no place for either Shakespeare or Byron, just as Dante and Michael Angelo are inconceivable in modern Italy which erected the ponderous monument to Victor Emmanuel and established Fascism. And herein lies the tragedy of both culture and civilization.

3

Every culture at a certain stage of its development discloses a principle which saps its own spiritual foundations. Culture is the development of the religious cult, of its differentiation and the unfolding of its content. Philosophy, science, architecture, painting, sculpture, music, poetry and morality are all integrally comprised in the ecclesiastical cult in an undifferentiated and undeveloped form. The Egyptian, the most ancient of cultures, began in the temple and the priests were its creators. Culture is also bound up with the ancestral cult and traditions. It is full of sacred symbols and signs of another spiritual reality. Every culture (even the material one) is spiritual and the product of the creative work of the spirit as applied to the natural elements. But culture develops a tendency to disintegrate in its religious and spiritual foundations and to repudiate its own symbolism. This is achieved through the process of 'enlightenment' which is common to both ancient and later Occidental culture. And this fact reveals the fatal dialectic inherent in culture. For at a certain stage of its existence, it begins to doubt and criticize the premises upon which it rests. It prepares its own destruction by separating itself from its sources. It exhausts itself spiritually and wastes its energies. It passes from the 'organic' to the 'critical' stage of its existence.

To understand the destiny of culture it is necessary to perceive its dynamic principles and fatal dialectic. Culture is the living process and destiny of peoples. But it becomes evident that it cannot maintain itself at the high peak of its efflorescence. Every type of culture known to history demonstrates its liability to disintegrate and be transformed into another state to which the term 'culture' is no longer applicable. And that is due to the fact that it develops a will to new 'life', to power and dominion at all costs. The will to power at all costs is the principle of civilization. The latter is always interested, whereas culture is disinterested in its highest achievements. Thus culture ends and civilization begins when the 'enlightened' reason sweeps away all spiritual obstacles in the way of the profits and enjoyments to be had from 'life' and when the will to power and organized dominion of life are strongest.

Civilization is the passage from culture, contemplation and the creation of values, to the experience of life itself whose torrent threatens to engulf man. Culture contains a principle which tends towards a practical-utilitarian and 'realistic', that is, civilizing achievement. Great philosophy and art as well as religious symbolism lose their significance and connection with 'life'. What had been considered the highest achievements of culture are now discredited. Its sacred and symbolic character are repudiated. Spiritual culture is proclaimed to be the illusion and self-deception of an enslaved consciousness, the phantasmal product of a badly organized society. The organization and technique of life are destined ultimately to emancipate mankind from the illusion and deception of culture, and to lay the foundations of a 'real' civilization. The spiritual illusions of culture had been produced by the lack of organization and technique; but they are destined to vanish once civilization masters technique and organizes life.

Economic materialism is the typical philosophy of an age of civilization. It solves the mystery and reveals the inner pathos of civilization. Neither the sway of economics nor the abasement of spiritual life can be laid at its door. The domination of economics was already a reality which had turned spiritual culture into a mere figment before materialism had made a doctrine of it. Its ideology, indeed, is no more than the reflex of reality. It is essentially an ideology of an age of civilization, perhaps its most extreme ideology. Civilization is inevitably dominated by economics; for it is by its nature technical and conceives all ideology and spiritual culture as a mere figment or illusion. It exposes the phantasmal character of every ideology and spirituality. Civilization considers the organization of power and technique as the authentic approach to and realization of 'life'. As opposed to culture it is not religious; it represents the triumph of the 'enlightened' reason, but this latter turns out to be abstract and pragmatical. It is neither symbolic, hierarchical nor organic. It is realistic, democratic and mechanical. It does not seek symbolic, but 'realistic' achievements in life; it desires real life and not the similitudes or symbols of other worlds. In Civilization, Capitalism and Socialism, collective labour stifles individual creation. Civilization de-personalizes. The emancipation of the personality, which civilization claims to achieve, is fatal to personal originality. The principle of personality is manifest only in culture. The will to power and 'life' destroys the personality. Such is the paradox of history.

4

The passage from culture to civilization implies a profound change in the relationship between man and nature, and thus in his social environment and ultimate destiny. Economic materialism pointed out this truth, but in a form peculiar to man's consciousness in a civilized age. The triumphant advent of the machine opened a new era in which life loses its organic character and natural rhythm; man is separated from nature by an artificial environment of machines, by the very instruments of his intended domination of nature. As a reaction against his mediaeval ascetic ideal, man puts aside both resignation and contemplation, and attempts to dominate nature, organize life and increase its productive forces. This, however, does not help to bring him into closer communion with the inner life and soul of nature. On the contrary, by mastering it technically and organizing its forces man becomes further removed from it. Organization proves to be the death of the organism. Life becomes increasingly a matter of technique. The machine sets its stamp upon the human spirit and all its manifestations. Thus civilization has neither a natural nor a spiritual, but a mechanical foundation. It represents *par excellence* the triumph of technique over both the spirit and organism. Its speculation and art tend to become increasingly technical in character. Futurist art is as characteristic of civilization as symbolist art of culture. The predominance of gnosiological, methodological and pragmatical currents in philosophy are also its peculiar feature. The very idea of an 'applied' philosophy is born of the will to power and desire to discover its principle. Civilization, too, develops the principle of specialization at the expense of the integrity of spiritual culture. All men become specialists and exercise specialized functions.

The machine and technique are the product of the mental development and discoveries of culture; but they sap its organic foundations and kill its spirit. Culture, having lost its soul, becomes civilization. Spiritual matters are discounted; quantity displaces quality. The assertion of the will to 'life', power, organization and earthly happiness, brings about mankind's spiritual decline; for the higher spiritual life is based upon asceticism and resignation. Such are the tragedy and fate of historical destinies. Knowledge and science become the instrument of realizing the will to power, earthly happiness and the triumph of technique whose sole aim is the enjoyment of life in its immediate manifestations. Art, too, becomes an instrument of technique and a decorative element in the organization of life. The whole beauty of culture associated with its temples and palaces now becomes a lifeless museum exhibit. The museum is the only tie civilization has with the past. There springs up a cult of life which

[216]

has no regard for any deeper purpose behind it. Nothing has an authentic value any longer. No moment or experience of life is sufficiently profound to permit of communion with eternity. Every instant and experience is but the means for speeding up the life processes aspiring towards a false eternity and the all-devouring vampire of the future, the promise of power and happiness. The ever-quickening *tempo* of civilization destroys all notion of either past, present or eternity.

Civilization as opposed to culture, which is given up to the contemplation of eternity, tends to be futurist. Machinery and technique are chiefly responsible for the speeding up of life and its exclusive aspiration towards the future. Organic life is slower, less impetuous, and more concerned with essentials, while civilized life is superficial and accidental; for it puts the means and instruments of life before the ends whose significance is lost. The consciousness of civilized men is concentrated exclusively upon the means and technique of life considered as the only reality, while its aims are regarded as illusory. Technique, organization and the productive processes are a reality while spiritual culture is unreal, a mere instrument of technique. The relation between the ends and the means is reversed and perverted. Everything is sacrificed to 'life', and its growing power, organization and enjoyment. But what is the purpose of 'life'? Has life any end or significance? This loss of any sense of purpose is the death of a culture. The machine acquires a magic power over man. But the romantic repudiation of the machine and civilization as merely a stage in human destiny and a trial fortifying the human spirit is helpless to improve matters, for a simple revival of culture is impossible. In an age of civilization culture

[217]

is always romantic and turned towards communion with past religious-organic epochs. This is a law. The classical style is impossible in civilization. All the best representatives of culture in the nineteenth century were romantics. But the only real way to culture lies through religious transfiguration.

5

Civilization is by its nature 'bourgeois' in the deepest spiritual sense of the word. 'Bourgeois' is synonymous precisely with the civilized kingdom of this world and the civilized will to organized power and enjoyment of life. The spirit of civilization is that of the middle classes; it is attached and clings to corrupt and transitory things; and it fears eternity. To be a bourgeois is therefore to be a slave of matter and an enemy of eternity. The perfected European and American civilizations gave rise to the industrial-capitalist system, which represents not only a mighty economic development but the spiritual phenomenon of the annihilation of spirituality. The industrial Capitalism of civilization proved to be the destroyer of the eternal spirit and the sacred traditions. Modern capitalist civilization is essentially atheistic and hostile to the idea of God. The crime of killing God must be laid at its door rather than at that of revolutionary Socialism, which merely adapted itself to the civilized 'bourgeois' spirit and accepted its negative heritage.

Industrial-capitalist civilization, it is true, did not altogether repudiate religion: it was prepared to admit its pragmatical utility and necessity. Thus religion, which had found a symbolic expression in culture, became pragmatical in civilization. It could, indeed, prove useful and practical in the organization and fostering of life. Civilization is by its nature

[218]

pragmatical. The popularity of pragmatism in America, the classical land of civilization, need cause no surprise. Socialism, on the other hand, repudiated pragmatical religion; but it pragmatically defends atheism as being more useful for the development of life forces and the worldly satisfaction of the larger masses of mankind. But the pragmatical and utilitarian approach of Capitalism had been the real source of atheism and spiritual bankruptcy. The useful and practically effective god of Capitalism cannot be the true God. He can be easily unmasked. Socialism is negatively right. The God of religious revelations and symbolic culture had long vanished from capitalist civilization, just as it had receded from Him. It had turned its back upon everything ontological; it is, in fact, anti-ontological, mechanistic and fictitious. Its automatism, technique and mechanism constitute an antithesis to the organic, cosmic and spiritual character of all being. Man's economic life is not in itself either mechanical or fictitious: it has real and divine roots in life; for man has both a duty and impulse to develop himself economically. But the divorce of economy from life, the exaltation of economics as the high principle of life, the technical interpretation of life, and the fundamental capitalist principle of profit transform man's economic life into a fiction. The capitalist system is sowing the seeds of its own destruction by sapping the spiritual foundation of man's economic life. Labour loses all spiritual purpose and justification and, as a result, brings an indictment against the whole system. Socialism is the penalty it pays. But Socialism carries on the work of civilization and reflects its 'bourgeois' principles; it attempts to develop civilization still further without infusing it with a new spirit. Thus industrial civilization manufactures fictions, inevitably saps both the spiritual discipline and motivating principle of labour and, in this way, prepares its own downfall.

Civilization is powerless to realize its dream of everlasting aggrandizement. The tower of Babylon will remain unfinished. The World War already illustrates the downfall of European civilization, the crash of the industrial system and the unmasking of the fictions which had nourished the 'bourgeois' world. Such is the tragic dialectic of historical destiny. Both culture and civilization are based upon it. Only a dynamic approach can help us to understand everything. And only then will it be seen that everything in historical destiny has a tendency to be transformed into its opposite, that everything is riddled with contradictions and carries the seeds of its own destruction.

Imperialism is the technical product of civilization. It is not culture. It is the bare will to universal domination and organization. It forms part of the capitalist system and is by nature technical. Such is the English and German 'bourgeois' imperialism of the nineteenth and twentieth centuries. It must be distinguished from the divine imperialisms of the past, from the Holy Roman and the Byzantine Empires, which were symbolic and belong to culture rather than civilization. Imperialism discloses the insurmountable dialectic of historical destiny. Its will to universal domination disintegrates and melts the historical bodies of the national states belonging to culture. The British Empire is the end of England as a national state. But the ravenous imperial will contains the seed of death. Imperialism in its uncontrollable development undermines its own foundations and prepares the transition to Socialism, which is likewise governed by the will to universal power and organization and which thus is only a further stage and manifestation of civilization. Both Imperialism and Socialism are the expression of a deep cultural crisis. They represent the triumph of civilization at the expense of culture. This does not imply that culture is dying out, for in its deeper sense it is eternal. Ancient culture has collapsed and seemingly died. But in fact it continues to live in us as a deep stratum in our being. And similarly, in an age of civilization, culture lives a qualitative and not quantitative life in our depths. Civilization brings with it barbarism, the vulgarization or loss of the perfect forms contributed by culture. This process of barbarization has several aspects. Thus an epoch of early mediaeval barbarism had succeeded the age of Hellenic culture and universal Roman civilization. This elemental barbarism was the result of the new blood that had been infused into the ancient civilization by the new peoples fresh from the northern forests. But the barbarism to which the high perfection of European and world civilization can give rise is of another kind. It is a barbarism tainted by machine-oil and all the defects of a technical civilization. Such is the dialectic peculiar to civilization. It exhausts man's spiritual energy and the sources of culture. And this finally introduces the reign not of natural and barbarian forces in the best sense of the word, but of magic automatism and mechanism as a substitute for authentic being. Civilization was born of man's will to real 'life', power and happiness as opposed to the symbolic and contemplative nature of culture. This technical transfiguration of life is one of the paths leading from culture to 'life' and its transfiguration. Man was destined to follow it in order to discover fully all his technical potentialities. But this path does not lead to authentic being and it only helps to destroy man's image.

6

A different type of will to 'life' and its transfiguration may spring up within a culture. Civilization is not the only possible passage from culture with its tragic antithesis to 'life' and its transfiguration. There is also the path of a religious transfiguration of life and fulfilment of true being. We can establish four periods or states in man's historical destiny: barbarism, culture, civilization and religious transfiguration. These states cannot be examined exclusively from the standpoint of chronology; for they can co-exist; they represent, in fact, the different predispositions of the human spirit. But one of these states tends to predominate at a given epoch. Thus the Hellenistic age and that of universal Roman civilization were destined to give birth to the will to religious transfiguration. And this accounts for the origin of Christianity, whose essential mission was to transfigure life. In doing so it achieved miracles; the will to perform miracles is always intimately connected with the will to bring about an authentic transfiguration of life. But historically Christianity passed through periods of barbarism, culture and civilization, although in them all it still represented essentially a transfiguration of life. In its culture Christianity was pre-eminently symbolic, contributing similes, symbols and images of transfiguration. In its period of civilization it became mainly pragmatical, the means of developing the processes of life and the technique of spiritual discipline. But on the peaks of civilization its will to miracle grew weak and died out. Civilized Christians still profess a lukewarm belief in past miracles, but they expect them no longer and have lost all fervent will to achieve the transfiguring miracle.

But this fervent will to miracle and the organic-spiritual transfiguration of life should reappear and inspire a dying culture with another sort of life than that offered it by a mechanical and technical civilization. Religion cannot remain a mere part of life, shelved and neglected. It must achieve that true ontological transfiguration of life which culture attains only symbolically and civilization technically. But we have, perhaps, still in store for us a period of aerial civilization.

Russia was a country of enigmatical destiny harbouring the passionate thought of a religious transfiguration of life. Our will to culture was always accompanied by the will to 'life'. It had two aspects which were often confused: a striving after a social transfiguration of life in civilization and after a religious transfiguration, a miracle in the destinies of human society or a people. We are facing the crisis of culture without having fully experienced the latter. Russians have always tended to be dissatisfied with culture as an intermediate stage of existence. Pushkin and the Alexandrian age constitute the peak of Russian culture. The Russian literature and thought of the later nineteenth century were no longer representative of culture, but rather of an urge to 'life' and religious transfiguration. That was the case of Gogol, Tolstoy and Dostoievsky as well as of Soloviev, Leontiev and Fedorov; and that, too, was the character of the more recent religious-philosophical currents. Our cultural traditions had always been too weak. As a result we are creating an ugly civilization, for the barbarian element in us is always strong and our will to religious transfiguration stricken with a sort of diseased vision. But the Russian consciousness is more acutely and deeply aware of the cultural crisis and tragedy of historical destiny than that of the more fortunate people of the West. The Russian soul has, perhaps, also a greater capacity for asserting its will to achieve the miracle of religious trans-figuration. Like all the peoples of the world to-day we lack culture and are destined to tread the path of civilization. But we shall never be so hide-bound by either cultural symbolism or the pragmatism of civilization as the peoples of the West. The will of the Russian people has need of purification and tempering; and our people has a great expiation in store for it. Only then will its will to transfigure life give it the right to determine its mission in the world.